NORTH AMERICAN GAME BIRDS

THE HUNTING & FISHING LIBRARY®

By Mike Hehner, Chris Dorsey and Greg Breining

MIKE HEHNER, a lifelong bird hunter and bird watcher, works as a Book Development Leader for *The Hunting & Fishing Library*. He is also an accomplished photographer, specializing in waterfowl and other game birds.

CHRIS DORSEY is Executive Editor of *Ducks Unlimited* magazine. He has authored five books and numerous magazine articles, primarily on waterfowl and upland bird hunting.

GREG BREINING is Managing Editor for *The Minnesota Volunteer*, published by the Minnesota Department of Natural Resources. He has written several books and numerous magazine articles on a wide variety of outdoor topics.

COWLES
Creative Publishing, Inc.

President/COO: Nino Tarantino
Executive V.P./Editor-in-Chief: William B. Jones

NORTH AMERICAN GAME BIRDS

Authors: Mike Hehner, Chris Dorsey, Greg Breining
Executive Editor, Outdoors Group: Don Oster
Hunting and Fishing Library Director: Dick Sternberg
Book Development Leader: Mike Hehner
Senior Editor: Bryan Trandem
Project Manager: Denise Bornhausen
Senior Art Director: Dave Schelitzche
Art Director: Linda Schloegel
Photo Editor: Anne Price
Researchers: Dave Maas, Jim Moynagh
V.P. Development, Planning and Production: Jim Bindas
Production Manager: Stasia Dorn
Copy Editor: Janice Cauley
Senior Desktop Publishing Specialist: Joe Fahey
Desktop Publishing Specialist: Laurie Kristensen
Production Staff: Mike Schauer
Cover Photo: Bill Marchel
Contributing Photographers: Denver Bryan, Dembinsky Photo Associates, Ellis Nature Photography, The Green Agency, Mike Hehner, Gary Kramer, Lon E. Lauber, William Lindner, Steve Maas, Bill Marchel, Dr. Scott Neilsen, B. "Moose" Peterson, Ron Spomer, Tom Stack and Associates, Keith Szafranski, Bill Thomas, U.S. Fish & Wildlife Service, Vireo, Visuals Unlimited, The Wild-life Collection, The Wildside of Life, Lovett Williams, Gary Zahm
Cooperating Individuals and Agencies: American Birding Association – Diana Bittner; Arizona Game and Fish Department – Ron Engel-Wilson; Ducks Unlimited – Ray Alisauskas, Dr. Bruce Batt, Dr. Jeff Nielsen, Dr. Jack Payne, John Takakawa; Keith Hansen; Tim Leary; Minnesota Department of Natural Resources – Jeff Lawrence; National Wild Turkey Federation – Mary Kennamer; Nevada Department of Wildlife – Norm Saake; North Dakota Tourism –

Dawn Charging; United States Fish and Wildlife Service – Keith Morehouse, Tom Nebel, Mark Newcastle, Nan Rollinson, Jerry Serie

Printed on American paper by: R. R. Donnelley & Sons Co.
00 99 98 97 / 5 4 3 2 1

Library of Congress Cataloging-in-Publication Data

Dorsey, Chris, 1965-
North American game birds / by Chris Dorsey, Greg Breining & Mike Hehner.
p. cm. – (The Hunting & fishing library)
Includes index.
ISBN 0-86573-049-0 (hardcover)
1. Game and game-birds–North America. 2. Fowling–North America.
I. Breining, Greg. II. Hehner, Mike III. Title. IV. Series.
SK313.D67 1996
799.2'4'097–dc20   95-39431

Contents

Introduction

This unique reference guide differs from other bird-identification books in that it focuses on the species of interest to bird hunters – upland game birds, waterfowl and shorebirds. Yet, with its spectacular color photos and in-depth biological information, it will appeal to any bird watcher.

Most of the photographs are the work of well-known wildlife photographers, including Dr. Scott Nielsen,

Bill Marchel, Gary Kramer and Rich Kirchner. In most cases, the birds are pictured in their natural surroundings.

The book covers every popular North American game bird, from favorites like the Canada goose to little-known birds like the sora. You'll learn how to identify each bird and how to distinguish them from similar species, both in the hand and on the wing.

Also described are any seasonal coloration differences for each species, as well as differences between males, females and juveniles. For accurate duck identification, you'll find a detailed wing chart with actual wing photographs rather than the usual drawings.

Besides a wealth of biological information, including size, food habits, migrational patterns, habitat, breeding behavior, social interaction and population trends, you'll also learn the basic techniques used for hunting each bird, as well as a rating of table quality.

Detailed range maps show you exactly where to find the birds. In the case of migratory species, you'll see where they breed and spend the summer, and where they winter. A color key for the range maps is shown at right.

Whether you're an avid hunter or just enjoy watching wildlife, this book is sure to gain a prominent space on your bookshelf.

KEY TO GAME BIRD RANGE

■ = breeding range

■ = breeding & wintering range

□ = wintering range

Waterfowl
Order Anseriformes

All waterfowl are ideally suited for a life spent in and around water. Webbed feet give them extraordinary swimming ability, and their long necks and broad, flattened bills allow them to feed on aquatic plant and animal life. Waterproof plumage and thick layers of insulating down keep these birds from losing body heat in cold water.

The order *Anseriformes* can be divided into five categories: geese and swans, puddle ducks, diving ducks, mergansers and sea ducks.

Geese and swans (pages 8 to 19) are distinguished mainly by their large size, with some approaching 20 pounds. During the migration, geese may form enormous flocks numbering in the tens of thousands. They fly in V-shaped formations to reduce wind resistance. Geese and swans exhibit no coloration differences between the sexes. They rarely breed before their second year. Geese may live 25 years; swans, 45. Geese and swans mate for life and maintain stronger family bonds than do ducks, with both parents caring for the young.

Ducks differ from swans and geese in that sexes usually vary in coloration. Males have distinctive, color-

ful plumage, while females are camouflaged with mottled, drab-brown colors. Pair bonds are temporary, with the drake deserting the female shortly after breeding. Most ducks are short-lived, but a few have been known to live 15 years.

Puddle ducks (pages 20 to 41), also known as dabblers, include some of the most widely hunted species, such as mallards and wood ducks. They feed on or just below the surface, either skimming food or tipping up, with feet and rump pointing skyward. Puddle ducks are adept at walking and feeding on land. They can take flight almost instantly by jumping straight into the air, from land or water.

Diving ducks (pages 42 to 53) have legs and feet positioned far back on their bodies. Rather awkward on land, they spend most of their time in the water.

They eat more invertebrates and fish than do puddle ducks, and feed by diving below the surface. Unlike puddle ducks, diving ducks must run a short distance across the water before taking flight. They usually fly in a straight line, often just a few feet off the surface of the water.

Mergansers (pages 54 to 56) are distinguished from the other ducks by their narrow, pointed bill with serrated edges, and their crested heads. Often called *fish ducks*, they feed primarily on minnows and other small fish.

Sea ducks (pages 57 to 63) spend much of their lives on the ocean. Expert divers, they have been known to reach depths of 200 feet to feed on mollusks, crustaceans and fish.

Canada Goose

(Branta canadensis)

Common Names – Canada, honker.

Important Subspecies – Biologists disagree on the number of subspecies, but some say there are more than a dozen. The largest is the giant Canada *(B. canadensis maxima);* the smallest, the cackling goose *(B. canadensis minima).*

Description – The legs, feet, tail, head and bill are black; the rump, a prominent white. The back, wings, sides and breast range from brown to gray, and the neck is black with white cheek patches extending around the throat. Giant Canadas often have a whitish patch on the crown. Cackling geese are distinguished by their stubby bill.

Size – Canada geese vary in size according to subspecies. Cackling geese average 3 pounds and measure about 24 inches long; giant Canadas, 11 pounds and 40 inches. Males are slightly larger than females.

Migration – Canada geese breed throughout most of Canada and Alaska, and across much of the northern United States. Fall migration begins when the waters in the breeding range freeze up – as early as September for birds in arctic regions, and as late as November for those in the United States.

The birds winter across most of the United States, and along the coast of British Columbia. Some winter as far south as northern Mexico. Most arrive on their wintering grounds from late October into January.

Habitat – In the North, the preferred breeding habitat is tundra. In the United States, Canadas breed around marshes and other bodies of water, often close to human development. They winter on any open water close to feeding fields.

Canada goose and cackling goose (inset)

Canada geese with young

Food Habits – These birds feed mostly on grains, grasses, alfalfa and clover. They generally fly to feeding fields in the morning and late afternoon, spending the rest of the day on water.

Breeding – Canada geese usually begin breeding in their third year, and they breed earlier in the season than any other waterfowl species. They prefer nesting sites surrounded by water, and will nest on islands, the tops of muskrat houses, floating tires and washtubs, and other man-made nesting platforms.

The female lays 4 to 7 whitish eggs, which hatch in about 27 days. If a clutch does not hatch successfully, the birds sometimes nest again, although the survival rate of the second clutch is low. Once mating

pairs are established, the birds remain together for life, but if one partner dies, the survivor seeks a new mate.

Social Interaction – Canada geese fly in family groups, often joining other families to form migration flocks ranging in size from a dozen to several hundred birds. Family units usually remain together through the first year, dispersing when nesting begins.

Highly vocal birds, Canadas have a variety of distinctive calls, the most common being the familiar "her-onk, her-onk," which can be heard at a considerable distance. Cackling geese, as their name suggests, have a recognizable cackle.

Population – Increasing. This bird has benefited from increased grain production along its migration

routes. Transplanting efforts by game managers have established new breeding flocks in areas where they previously did not exist. Canada geese thrive in urban settings, and some cities have such large goose populations that the birds are considered a nuisance.

Hunting Strategies – The most common technique is placing decoys in feeding fields and calling the birds as they fly out to feed in morning and late afternoon. They can also be hunted by setting floating decoys in waters the birds use for resting. Around refuge areas, hunters often pass-shoot birds as they leave or return.

Eating Quality – Good; the meat is mild-flavored but can be tough.

Snow Goose

(Anser caerulescens)

Common Names – Snow, wavie.

Important Subspecies – Two are recognized: the greater snow goose (*A. caerulescens atlantica*) and the lesser snow goose (*A. caerulescens caerulescens*).

Description – Lesser snow geese may sport either dark or white plumage. Dark-phase birds, called *blues*, and white-phase birds, called *snows*, are the same species, though they were once considered separate.

White-phase birds have white plumage, except for the black primary wing feathers, which are easily seen in flight. Dark-phase birds are dark gray overall, with a white head and upper neck.

In both phases, the legs and feet are reddish, and the bill is pink, with black crescents along the sides. By fall, juveniles resemble adults.

Greater snows resemble white-phase lessers, but are slightly larger. They do not exhibit a dark phase.

Size – Adult lesser snows measure 27 to 31 inches long and weigh 5 to 7 pounds; adult greaters, 28 to 33 inches long and 6 to 8½ pounds. Males are slightly larger than females.

Migration – Lesser snows breed along the shores of Hudson Bay and across subarctic Canada. The fall migration begins in late September, and by early November most birds are en route to the wintering grounds.

The Gulf Coast from Louisiana to northern Mexico is the major wintering area for lesser snows, but they also winter in scattered areas along the western coasts of the United States and Mexico. Smaller pockets of birds are scattered across the western states. By the end of December, most have arrived on the wintering grounds.

Greater snows breed on several of the arctic islands and in Greenland. The fall migration begins in late August, with birds stopping over on the St. Lawrence River before continuing south. They winter along the Atlantic seaboard from New Jersey through North Carolina, arriving in late November to late December.

Habitat – Snow geese breed on tundra habitat with shrubs, marsh grasses and bulrushes for cover.

Greater snows nest within a few miles of the coast. Snow geese winter on coastal bays and marshes, near a food source. Lesser snows may also winter on freshwater marshes.

Food Habits – On the breeding grounds, snow geese feed mainly on grasses. On the wintering grounds, greater snows eat mostly cord grass and bulrushes, as well as some small grains. Lesser snows feed more heavily on small grains, mainly corn and wheat. They also eat alfalfa and winter wheat.

Breeding – Snows begin breeding at age 3 or 4. Breeding takes place during the spring migration, before the birds have reached their nesting areas.

The female builds her makeshift nest on tundra near water. Repeat nesters usually return to the same nest site used the previous season. The female scrapes out a shallow depression in the tundra and lines it with down. She lays 4 to 5 whitish eggs, which hatch in 23 to 24 days. The male guards the nesting site to drive off intruders, and both parents stay with the young through the fall migration.

The color phases of the lesser snow do not breed true. White-phase parents can produced dark-phase offspring, and vice versa.

Social Interaction – Lesser snows migrate in enormous flocks of up to a thousand birds. Greater snows migrate in much smaller flocks, sometimes only a few dozen birds. Both subspecies winter in flocks numbering in the tens of thousands. Snow geese are noisy birds that make a series of high-pitched yelps. At close range, the noise of a flock can be deafening.

Population – Increasing. Lesser snow numbers have risen because of improved habitat along the migration routes and better disease control on refuges. Greater snows were overhunted in the early 1900s, so the hunting season was closed. By 1975, numbers had rebounded and the season was reopened. Since then, numbers have continued to increase.

Hunting Strategies – The best hunting is near refuges where the geese stop during the fall migration. The birds normally roost on refuge waters, moving into grain fields in the early morning and late afternoon.

Lesser snows migrate in large flocks, so hunters often use several hundred decoys, along with high-pitched calls. Older birds are warier and more difficult to lure with decoys. Decoying is also difficult if there is a massive flock of live geese nearby.

Greater snows are hunted on tidal marshes and in crop fields. Because they fly in smaller flocks, they are more easily attracted by decoys and goose calls.

Eating Quality – Fair; the meat is dark and can be somewhat strong-tasting, especially in older birds.

Juvenile dark-phase lesser snow goose (left), adult white-phase (center), adult dark-phase (right)

Greater White-Fronted Goose
(Anser albifrons)

Common Names – Speck, specklebelly, whitefront, laughing goose.

Description – The head, neck and back are brownish gray; the tail, black. The undersides are whitish with dark brown speckles. A distinctive white facial patch rings the base of the pinkish bill. The legs and feet are orange. Males and females are similar in appearance. Juveniles resemble adults, but lack the white facial ring and dark brown belly spots.

Size – Adults measure 26 to 31 inches long and weigh 4½ to 7 pounds. Males are slightly larger than females.

Migration – The breeding range includes the Canadian Arctic and large portions of Alaska. Whitefronts are among the earliest migrants, leaving the breeding grounds from mid-August to early October. Flying with few stops, they arrive on the wintering grounds from late September to November.

Main wintering areas include California's Central Valley and the Gulf coast from Louisiana to central Mexico.

Habitat – During the nesting season, white-fronted geese prefer to be near water, on tundra habitat with low-growing plants. While on the wintering grounds, the birds roost in salt marshes, and use agricultural fields and grasslands for feeding and loafing.

Food Habits – The birds eat grasses, sedges and horsetail while on the nesting areas. On the wintering areas, they feed mainly on bulrushes, rice, wheat, corn and grasses.

Breeding – Whitefronts normally don't breed until they are 3 years old. The female builds a shallow nest, usually in tall grass along a tidal slough or sedge marsh, and lines it with down and vegetation. An average clutch consists of 5 cream- or buff-colored eggs, which hatch in 23 to 25 days. Within 24 hours

after the eggs hatch, the male leads the brood to water.

Social Interaction – These geese have strong family bonds. The juveniles often remain with the parents until the next nesting season. White-fronted geese can be easily identified by their unique "atta-luk, atta-luk" calls.

Population – Increasing; numbers have shown an upward trend since the late 1960s, mainly because of better management practices and improved habitat along the migration routes.

Hunting Strategies – You can buy calls and decoys designed for whitefronts, but the birds also respond to snow goose or Canada goose decoys and calls.

Because they share the same refuges and feeding grounds as Canadas and snows, many whitefronts are taken incidentally by hunters seeking those birds.

Eating Quality – Excellent; white-fronted geese are among the mildest and best-tasting of all North American geese.

Flock of Ross' geese with a rare blue-phase bird. Inset compares Ross' goose (left) and lesser snow goose (right).

Ross' Goose
(Anser rossii)

Common Names – Horned wavie, little wavie, warty-nosed wavie.

Description – The Ross' goose resembles the lesser snow goose, but is smaller and has a stubbier bill. Ross' geese often travel with snow geese and can easily be identified in flight by their faster wing beat.

Like the lesser snow goose, the Ross' goose has two color phases: the common white phase and a much less common dark phase. The dark phase resembles the dark-phase snow goose, but the dark plumage extends farther up the neck. In the white phase, the body is white with black primary wing feathers. In both phases the legs and feet are reddish and the bill is pink. By fall, the juveniles resemble the adults.

Size – Adults measure 22 to 26 inches long and weigh 3 to 4 pounds. Males are slightly larger than females.

Migration – Ross' geese breed in the central Arctic region of Canada. They are early migrants, leaving the breeding grounds by late September, and reaching the wintering ground by mid-December. Most winter in California, with pockets of wintering birds

in New Mexico and along the Gulf Coast of Texas and Louisiana.

Habitat – In the nesting season, the birds prefer tundra habitat along a river or small lake. During migration and while on their wintering grounds, they favor fresh or saltwater marshes with nearby grasslands and agricultural fields.

Food Habits – In spring and summer, these geese feed mainly on grasses. During migration and while on the wintering grounds, they also feed on rice, wheat and barley.

Breeding – Most birds do not breed until their third year. In a small colony segregated from nonbreeding birds, the female uses twigs and vegetation to build a nest near rocks, trees or other protection. She lays about 4 white eggs, which hatch in

approximately 22 days. Both the male and female guard the goslings.

Social Interaction – Juveniles remain with the family through their first year, until the parents begin to incubate a new clutch of eggs. In August, the birds gather in large flocks to molt. When migrating, they often mix with snow geese. Ross' geese make high-pitched "kek-ke-gak" calls.

Population – Increasing; numbers have climbed steadily since the 1950s, due mainly to improved game-management practices along the migration routes.

Hunting Strategies – Most birds are taken incidentally by snow goose hunters using decoys and calls.

Eating Quality – Fair; the meat is dark and similar to that of snow goose.

Tundra Swan
(Cygnus columbianus)

Common Name – Whistling swan.

Description – Sometimes confused with snow geese, these birds are larger, with much longer necks. They are completely white, including the wing tips, and have black legs and feet. Juveniles are brownish gray, with a pinkish bill and grayish legs and feet.

Size – Adults measure 47 to 58 inches long and weigh 10½ to 18½ pounds. Males are usually larger than females.

Migration – Tundra swans breed along the arctic coast of the Northwest Territories, the Yukon, and in northern and western Alaska. They begin the fall migration in September and October, reaching their wintering grounds by November and December. The birds winter along the Atlantic and Pacific coasts of the United States, in southern Texas, western Nevada and portions of the Rocky Mountain states.

Habitat – The birds breed on coastal tundra, and on inland tundra, generally near ponds or small lakes. They winter on coastal bays and on fresh- and salt-water marshes.

Food Habits – Tundra swans tip up to feed, using their long necks to reach aquatic plants. In winter, they also feed on corn and other small grains.

Breeding – Although little is known about the tundra swan's breeding habits, it is believed that they do not breed until they are at least 3 years old.

The female typically builds her elaborate, down-lined nest on an elevated area of tundra within a few feet of a lake or pond. She lays 4 to 5 creamy white eggs, which hatch in 27 to 31 days. The male helps guard the nest and tend the young.

Social Interaction – In mid-August, many families join together on coastal waters or inland lakes, forming pre-migration flocks of 30 to 100 birds. Family groups stay together through the fall migration.

Although it is called a *whistling swan*, the tundra swan makes sounds better described as honks. In flight, it makes a three-note "wow-wow-wow" call.

Population – Stable; the bird is well protected and can be hunted only in a handful of states and provinces.

Hunting Strategies – Where hunting for tundra swans is allowed, it is done by pass-shooting or by setting white-painted magnum goose decoys in feeding fields or on the water.

Eating Quality – Fair; the meat is dark, and tends to be tough in older birds.

Pacific and Atlantic (inset) brant

Brant
(Branta bernicla)

Common Names – Sea goose, brent goose, white-bellied goose, black brant (Pacific subspecies).

Important Subspecies – Two are recognized: the Atlantic brant (*B. bernicla hrota*), and the Pacific brant (*B. bernicla nigricans*).

Description – With their unusually rapid wingbeat, brant in flight look more like ducks than geese. The head, neck and chest are black, and the sides of the neck are marked with white streaks. The undersides are whitish. Juveniles resemble adults. The subspecies are nearly identical, though the Pacific brant has darker undersides and more pronounced neck marks.

Size – Adults measure 22 to 26 inches and weigh 2¾ to 3½ pounds. Males are slightly larger than females.

Migration – The breeding range for the Pacific subspecies includes the arctic coast of Alaska, the Yukon, and the eastern Northwest Territories. Atlantic brant breed on the arctic islands of Canada.

The fall migration begins in late August, and by early October all birds have left the breeding grounds. Pacific brant, which migrate considerably farther than Atlantic birds, leave first. Flying nearly non-stop at speeds up to 62 miles per hour, the birds arrive on the wintering grounds between late October and late December.

The Pacific subspecies winters mainly in the Baja Peninsula and on the western coast of Mexico, while Atlantic birds winter along the eastern seaboard from Massachusetts to North Carolina.

Habitat – During the nesting season, brant prefer coastal islands or tundra habitat near water. In winter, they are found on coastal estuaries and saltwater marshes.

Food Habits – Where eelgrass still exists, it is the food of choice for brant. They also eat sea lettuce, wigeon grass, sedges and bulrushes.

Breeding – Like many species of geese, brant rarely breed before their third year. The hen builds a down-lined nest on a bed of matted sedges near the water's edge, then lays a clutch of 3 to 5 creamy white eggs. With the male close by, the hen incubates the eggs for 23 to 24 days before they hatch. The family structure is unusual among waterfowl species; the male leads the newly hatched brood with the female taking a secondary role.

Social Interaction – In early September, nonbreeding birds group up and begin migrating south. Family groups wait until mid-September before joining other families to form a migration flock of more than 100 birds. When flying or feeding, the birds emit a subtle, low-pitched "ronk-ronk" call.

Population – Stable. Numbers fell sharply in the 1930s, when disease wiped out eelgrass over much of the brant's range. But as the birds adjusted to feed on other plants, the population rebounded.

Hunting Strategies – You can pass-shoot brant as they fly into bays and lagoons to feed on weedy mud flats at low tide. They also respond to decoys, and can be hunted from low-profile sculling boats.

Eating Quality – Fair; the meat is very dark with a strong flavor.

Mallard
(Anas platyrhynchos)

Common Names – Greenhead (male), Susie (female), quacker.

Description – This puddle duck is one of the most recognized of all waterfowl species. The distinctive, colorful drake has an iridescent green head with an olive-green bill, a white neck ring and a rusty-colored breast. The belly and sides are silvery white; the back, gray.

The hen is mottled brown overall, with a lighter belly and darker back. Her bill is orange with black blotches. Both sexes have orange feet and legs, and a blue-violet speculum with white margins. Juveniles resemble adult females, but the young males begin to show adult colors by early fall.

Size – Drakes measure 20 to 28 inches long and weigh 2 to 4 pounds; hens, 18 to 25 inches long and 1½ to 3½ pounds.

Migration – Mallards have the most extensive breeding range of any North American duck, nesting through most of the United States, and from eastern Canada to northern Alaska. The largest breeding populations are found in the prairie pothole region of the United States and Canada.

Mallards move south only when freezing water forces them to leave. The largest wintering population is located in the south-central states and Mexico, although wintering birds can be found across most of the United States.

Habitat – During the nesting season, mallards prefer large sloughs and marshes, but they adapt easily to urban areas, often nesting in parks. In winter, mallards in the North are drawn to open-water rivers and lakes near agricultural fields. In the South, they are also found in wooded swamps.

Food Habits – In addition to corn, soybeans, wheat and other grains, mallards feed on rice and a wide variety of aquatic plants, including pondweeds, coontail, wild millet, sedges, canary grass, bulrushes

Mallard drake and hen (inset)

and smartweed. When migrating and while on the wintering grounds, mallards often feed in grain fields in the morning, move to ponds and wetlands to loaf in midday, then return to feed on grain in late afternoon.

Breeding – Mallards begin breeding in their first year. They are polygamous, and several drakes may attempt to breed with a single hen.

In an upland area, usually within 100 yards of water, the hen scrapes out a depression in dead vegetation, adding grass and twigs to complete the base of the nest. She lays 9 to 12 buff-colored eggs, cushioning

them with down plucked from her breast. The eggs hatch in about 28 days.

Social Interaction – After the drakes abandon the hens, they often congregate on large wetlands, where they remain during the molt. Hens stay with their young until they can fly; then, the family group joins the male flock, and the hens molt. By migration time, these combined flocks may number in the thousands.

Mallards are gregarious, highly vocal birds that call to entice other ducks into landing nearby. Both sexes make quacking sounds, although the hen's call is much louder and higher in pitch.

Population – Increasing; the low numbers seen during the drought-afflicted 1980s have risen steadily as water levels in the prairie pothole region improved.

Hunting Strategies – Mallards are the most popular of all waterfowl. Most hunters set decoys in wetlands and use mallard calls to lure the birds into shooting range. You may also have good hunting in flooded crop fields, which can draw in thousands of birds.

Eating Quality – Excellent; mallards have mild-tasting breast meat and are among the best-eating of all ducks.

American Black Duck
(Anas rubripes)

Common Names – Black, black mallard, red leg.

Description – This puddle duck is sometimes mistaken for the hen mallard, but is considerably darker and, at a distance, may look completely black. At close range, the black duck's overall color is brownish black, and the head and neck are a lighter brown.

The head has a dark streak running through the eye from the bill across the upper cheek. The speculum is blue with black edges, in contrast to the white-edged speculum on the mallard. The undersides of the wings are white.

The hen and drake are nearly identical, but the drake's bill is bright yellow with a dark center, while the hen's is olive-green. Both sexes have reddish orange legs and feet. Juvenile birds closely resemble adults, but the young male's bill lacks the dark center.

Mallards and black ducks sometimes hybridize, producing offspring with characteristics of both species.

Size – Adults measure 19 to 24 inches long and weigh 2 to 3½ pounds. Drakes are slightly larger than hens.

Migration – The primary breeding range includes the northern states from Minnesota eastward, as well as the eastern half of Canada. Black ducks begin the fall migration in September and October, normally reaching their wintering areas in November and December. Most birds winter along the Atlantic coast, from Maine to South Carolina, but smaller concentrations can be found in several other southern states. Some winter as far north as the Maritimes.

Habitat – Black ducks breed in brushy cover near fresh- or saltwater marshes. Most birds spend the winter on coastal bays and marshes, but some prefer open rivers and lakes.

Food Habits – Black ducks are equally at home feeding in freshwater and saltwater marshes. They eat many types of food, including crustaceans and aquatic plants, such as wigeon grass and eelgrass. They also feed on acorns and, occasionally, small grains.

Breeding – Like mallards, black ducks begin breeding in their first year. They like isolation, and vigorously defend their breeding territory.

The hen returns to the same nesting area each year, often choosing a location within a few yards of her previous nesting site. She scrapes a depression in the ground, then lines it with dead plant material. Black ducks also may nest on man-made platforms, on muskrat houses, or in the crotches of trees.

The hen lays about 9 creamy white eggs and cushions them with her own down. They hatch in about 26 days.

Social Interaction – After breeding, drakes group up on ponds or wetlands to molt. Hens stay with their young until mid- to late summer, then all the birds join the molting flock. Like mallards, black ducks form large wintering flocks. Their calls are similar to those of a mallard.

Population – Declining. Black duck numbers have been dwindling for many years. Some biologists believe the decline is the result of interbreeding with mallards, which weakens the black duck gene pool.

Hunting Strategies – Black ducks usually are hunted in and around coastal estuaries and bays, with the same techniques used for mallards. But because they are considerably warier, they may be more difficult to lure with decoys and calls.

Eating Quality – Excellent; the meat is similar in taste to that of mallard.

Northern Pintail

(Anas acuta)

Common Names – Spike, spiketail, sprig.

Description – Named for the drake's long, pointed tail feathers, this puddle duck has a long, thin in-flight profile that is unmistakable.

The drake's head and neck are chocolate brown, with a white stripe running up both sides of the neck. The chest, belly and throat are white. The back and sides are grayish, growing darker near the tail. The speculum is green.

The hen has an overall mottled brown color, with a light belly. Her bill is gray and her tail, though pointed, is not as long as the drake's. The speculum is brownish. Both sexes have dark gray legs and feet, and bluish gray bills. Juvenile birds resemble adult hens. By fall the young males begin to develop their adult plumage, although they lack the long tail.

Size – Drakes measure 23 to 30 inches long and weigh $1\frac{1}{2}$ to 3 pound; hens, 21 to 25 inches long and $1\frac{1}{3}$ to $2\frac{1}{2}$ pounds.

Migration – This bird's extensive breeding range is surpassed only by that of the mallard. Pintails breed across much of the western United States, Canada and Alaska, with the largest breeding population found in the prairie pothole region.

Pintails begin the fall migration in August, and by October or November most have reached their wintering grounds. They winter throughout the southern United States, the Caribbean islands, Mexico and parts of Central America.

Habitat – Favored breeding habitat is open wetlands, slow rivers and streams, and lakes with marshy shorelines. In winter, pintails prefer freshwater marshes and lakes, and coastal bays and estuaries.

Pintail drake and hen (inset)

Food Habits – Pintails feed heavily on rice and small grains, including wheat, oats and barley. They also eat invertebrates and many types of aquatic vegetation.

Like mallards, pintails often feed in crop fields in the morning, move to ponds and wetlands for the midday loafing hours, then return to feeding fields in the evening.

Breeding – Most pintails breed in their first year. Unlike most ducks, pintails prefer to nest in open areas with low vegetation, usually within 40 yards of water, but some nests may be a mile or more away.

The nest is a shallow depression scraped in the ground and lined with vegetation and down. The hen lays about 8 pale gray to olive-green eggs, which hatch in approximately 23 days.

Social Interaction – After breeding, the drakes congregate on a large wetlands to molt. The hens remain with their broods until the young can fly, then families join the males. Pintails form huge migration flocks, often mixing with mallards.

The drake has a distinct but subtle "preep-preep" whistle. The hen utters a series of low quacks, similar to those made by mallards.

Population – Declining; the extensive drought of the 1980s caused a drastic decline in population, and the bird's numbers have not yet rebounded.

Hunting Strategies – Pintails are hunted in much the same fashion as mallards. They readily respond to mallard decoys and calls, though pintail decoys and special pintail whistles are available.

Eating Quality – Excellent; the meat is similar in taste to that of mallard.

Gadwall drake

Gadwall
(Anas strepera)

Common Names – Gray
duck, gray mallard.

Description – The drake
gadwall is a subtly beautiful
puddle duck with gray-
barred side feathers, a white
belly and a black rump. The
speculum is white, framed by
black and brown feathers.
The bill is black.

The hen's back is brown; her sides, tan. The undersides are light, and the bill is dull orange with a gray
center streak. The white speculum is not as pronounced as the drake's. Both sexes have yellowish
orange legs and feet. Juveniles resemble adult hens,
but in late fall the young males develop their adult
plumage.

Size – Adults measure 18 to 22 inches long and
weigh 1½ to 2½ pounds. Drakes are slightly larger
than hens.

Migration – The prairie pothole region is the prime
breeding area for gadwalls, but breeding populations
can also be found in the Great Plains and Rocky
Mountain states, Alaska, and the eastern Great Lakes

Gadwall hen

area. The fall migration begins in September. Gadwalls generally fly at night, with most birds arriving on their wintering grounds in October and November. Louisiana is home to the largest population of wintering gadwalls, but the birds also winter throughout much of the south and most of the Atlantic and Pacific coastal states.

Habitat – The birds nest mainly around small prairie wetlands. In winter, they can be found on saltwater marshes and estuaries, and on freshwater marshes and rivers.

Food Habits – Favorite foods include the stems and leaves of aquatic plants, such as pondweeds, coontail, wigeon grass, muskgrass and eelgrass.

Breeding – Most birds breed during their first year. Because they migrate northward later than most other puddle-duck species, gadwalls are late nesters.

Typically, the hen chooses a nesting site in thick, tall vegetation near water, often on islands. She scrapes a shallow depression, lines it with dead vegetation and

down, then lays about 10 creamy white eggs, which hatch in approximately 24 days.

Social Interaction – After breeding, drakes leave their mates and congregate on nearby ponds to molt. After the young can fly, the rest of the birds join the molting flock. Gadwalls usually are found in small groups, and often mix with other puddle ducks. Although they are not particularly vocal, hens sometimes emit a mallardlike "gag-ag-ag-ag" call, and drakes may utter short "nheck" calls and low whistles.

Population – Increasing. Because gadwalls are secretive nesters, they have a high rate of nesting success. Their numbers remain strong even when other ducks are in decline.

Hunting Strategies – Gadwalls are often taken incidentally by mallard hunters. They readily respond to mallard decoys and calls.

Eating Quality – Excellent; the taste is similar to that of mallard.

American Wigeon
(Anas americana)

Common Names –
Baldpate, gray duck.

Description – This puddle
duck's common name,
baldpate, comes from the
drake's prominent white
forehead and crown.

The drake has a deep green
streak running from the eye
to the back of the head. The
back, sides and chest are
pinkish brown; the undersides, white. Pronounced
white shoulder patches are clearly visible in flight.

The hen's sides and chest are chestnut-colored; her
back, gray-brown. Both sexes have blue-gray legs
and feet. The bill is blue-gray with a black tip.
Juvenile birds resemble adult hens.

Size – Adults measure 18 to 23 inches long and
weigh 1 to 2½ pounds. Drakes are slightly larger
than hens.

Migration – The breeding range includes much of
Alaska, the western United States and western and
northern Canada. A small breeding population can
be found in upper New England.

These ducks are among the earliest fall migrants,
leaving the northern nesting grounds in mid-August
and reaching stopover areas by September. By
December most birds have arrived on the wintering
grounds.

Wintering birds can be found in all the coastal states,
as well as British Columbia and Mexico. The largest
wintering concentrations are in the Central Valley of
California and the extensive coastal marshes of
Louisiana.

American wigeon drake and hen (inset)

Habitat – Wigeon nest primarily around prairie
marshes, ponds and shallow lakes. During winter
they often are found on coastal bays and estuaries.

Food Habits – Wigeon feed mainly on stems and
leafy portions of aquatic plants. They also graze on
upland grasses and legumes.

Breeding – Wigeon begin breeding in their first
year. The hen typically nests in a clump of brushy
cover near water. She builds her nest using grasses
and down plucked from her own breast, then lays

8 or 9 creamy white eggs, which hatch in about 24 days.

Social Interaction – Wigeon may form small feeding groups. Unlike most puddle ducks, they seldom mix with other species. Shortly after the hens begin incubation, the drakes congregate on a large wetlands to molt. The hen remains with her young until they can fly, then all birds join the molting flock.

The drake wigeon emits a three-note "wh-ee-oo" whistling call. The hen is normally silent.

Population – Increasing. The drought of the 1980s greatly reduced wigeon numbers, but the population has risen steadily since then.

Hunting Strategies – The wigeon is a secondary target for mallard hunters, because it readily responds to mallard calls and decoy spreads.

Eating Quality – Excellent; the meat has a taste similar to that of mallard.

Wood Duck
(Aix sponsa)

Common Names – Woodie, acorn duck, summer duck, Carolina duck, squealer.

Description – Arguably the most beautiful of all North American puddle ducks, the drake wood duck has a ruddy red chest, and a blue, white, and iridescent green head with a pronounced crest. Its flanks are tawny; the underside, whitish. The bill is reddish overall, with a yellow ring at the base, a black tip, and a white patch on top.

The hen has a less pronounced crest. The bill is dull gray with a black tip, and the eye is circled by a white ring. Her back is dark brown, and the sides are mottled with tan and gray. The undersides are whitish. Both sexes have a blue speculum, and the legs and feet are yellow, though the color is duller in hens. Juveniles resemble adult hens, but in fall young males develop their adult plumage.

Size – Adults measure 15 to 21 inches long and weigh 1⅓ to 2 pounds. Drakes are slightly larger than hens.

Migration – The breeding range includes most of the eastern half of the United States, the west coast states, and portions of central Canada and British Columbia. Pockets of breeding birds are also found in the Great Plains states.

Wood ducks breeding in the South generally do not migrate, but birds in the northern part of the breeding range begin their fall migration in September, reaching their winter destinations by mid-November. Most eastern wood ducks spend the winter in the southeastern United States and into Mexico. In the West, most birds winter in the Sacramento Valley of California and along the western coast of Mexico.

Habitat – Wood ducks breed around marshes, rivers and ponds in densely wooded areas. In winter they prefer wooded wetlands.

Food Habits – Acorns from pin and white oaks are the preferred food of wood ducks. Lacking acorns, they will eat hickory nuts and seeds from a variety of other plants, including bald cypress, button bush, bur reed and arrow arum. They also feed on corn.

Breeding – Most wood ducks breed in their first year. The hen usually nests in a woodpecker hole or other tree cavity, which she lines with her own down. Wood ducks also nest in man-made nesting boxes (right).

The average clutch consists of about 12 beige eggs, although several hens may lay their eggs in the same nest. The hen incubates the eggs for about 30 days.

Man-made nesting box

Social Interaction – As hens undertake incubating duties, drakes sometimes congregate in nearby trees. Wood ducks rarely form massive flocks. Fall migration groups consist of 20 to 100 birds, although flocks on the winter feeding areas may be larger.

The hen utters a high-pitched "woo-eek" squeal. The drake makes a "jeeeEE" call, heard most often when he is flushed.

Population – Increasing. Near the turn of the century, wood ducks seemed headed for extinction as their forest habitat fell to agricultural development. The season was closed until the early 1940s. Thanks to reduced bag limits and the introduction of man-made nesting boxes, the population has rebounded dramatically. For the past several decades, wood ducks have ranked second only to mallards in total harvest.

Hunting Strategies – Prized for its striking beauty, the highly maneuverable wood duck poses a difficult target when flying through flooded timber. Jump-shooting is a popular technique around small rivers and ponds. Some hunters attract birds with wood duck decoys and wood duck whistles, or take them incidentally while hunting mallards.

Eating Quality – Excellent; the breast meat is tender and mild-tasting.

Wood duck hen (left) and drake (right)

Blue-Winged Teal

(Anas discors)

Common Names – Blue-wing, summer teal, rice rocket.

Description – Named for their blue wing patches, these puddle ducks are easy to identify by their small size and erratic flight. In breeding plumage, the drake has a striking white facial crescent, a green speculum and a gray-blue head. The bill is black. During the fall hunting season, however, when the drakes are just completing the molt, their colors are not fully developed.

The hen is an overall mottled brown, with a light brown belly and a grayish bill. Both sexes have yellow-to-orange legs and feet. Juveniles resemble adult hens, but by early fall the young males begin to develop their adult colors.

Size – Adults measure 14 to 16 inches long and weigh ½ to 1⅓ pounds. Drakes are slightly larger than hens.

Migration – The breeding range includes the northern half of the United States, many of the central states, parts of Alaska and much of southern Canada. The prairie pothole region contains the largest concentration of breeding birds. Bluewings are early migrants. Drakes head south from late August to early September, a few weeks before the hens. Most arrive on their wintering grounds in October and November.

In the United States, bluewings winter in California, the Gulf Coast states and Arkansas. Wintering birds are also found throughout Mexico and as far south as northern South America.

Habitat – The preferred nesting habitat is prairie grasslands near ponds and marshes. During the winter, bluewings are usually found on coastal backwaters.

Blue-winged teal hen (left) and drake (right)

Food Habits – The bluewing's diet consists mainly of aquatic plants, such as muskgrass, wigeon grass, coontail, duckweeds and pondweeds. They also eat aquatic invertebrates.

Breeding – Bluewings usually breed in their first year. They prefer to nest in fallow hay fields or other grassy cover well away from water. The hen scrapes a bowl-like depression in the ground and lines it with grasses and down. She lays about 10 creamy tan eggs, which hatch in approximately 24 days. The drake stays with the hen until the third week of incubation.

Social Interaction – After leaving their mates, the drakes congregate at nearby marshes and ponds to begin their molt. Hens remain with their broods until the ducklings can fly, then form their own molting flocks. These segregated flocks sometimes number 2,000 to 3,000 birds.

Drakes utter peeping notes, and the hens make light quacks.

Population – Increasing. Bluewing numbers are still below long-term averages because of the drought of the 1980s, but numbers have risen as water conditions in the prairie pothole region improved.

Hunting Strategies – Use the same techniques as for mallards: position decoys on a shallow marsh or pond, then conceal yourself in nearby cover and wait for the birds to approach within shooting distance. Jump-shooting can also be effective.

Eating Quality – Excellent; the meat is tender and mild-tasting.

Green-Winged Teal
(Anas crecca)

Green-winged teal hen

Common Names – Green-wing, common teal.

Description – This species is the smallest of all North American puddle ducks. The drake has a rusty head with a brilliant green patch running from the eye down the neck. A green speculum marks the wing. The buff chest is flecked with brown and is

framed by a white bar that separates the chest from the gray back and sides.

The undersides are white; the legs and feet, brownish gray; the bill, dark gray. During the fall, when the drakes are completing the molt, their colors are not yet fully developed.

The hen has mottled brown plumage overall, with white undersides. Juveniles resemble adult females, but by late fall the young males develop their adult colors.

Size – Adults measure 13 to 15 inches long and weigh ½ to 1 pound.

Migration – The breeding range includes most of Alaska and Canada, and the prairie pothole region of the United States. Unlike bluewings, greenwings often stay on their northern breeding grounds until late fall. They prefer to migrate at night, traveling in flocks of 100 or more birds. Most arrive on the wintering grounds in late November.

The winter range includes most of the southern United States, the Pacific Northwest, some of the Rocky Mountain and eastern seaboard states, and most of Mexico.

Habitat – The preferred nesting habitat is prairie grassland with marshes and ponds. They also nest on

tundra and around northern lakes in forested areas. In winter, the birds favor coastal estuaries and bays.

Food Habits – Greenwings do most of their feeding on mud flats bordering wetlands. They eat seeds of moist-soil plants, such as smartweeds, nutgrasses and millets, but also feed on seeds from a variety of aquatic plants, including bulrushes, spike rushes and pondweeds.

Breeding – The greenwing normally breeds during its first year. A secretive nester, the hen chooses a nesting site 50 to 100 feet from water, in a clump of dense grass or brushy cover. After constructing a grass nest and lining it with down, she lays 8 or 9 creamy white eggs, which hatch in about 21 days.

Social Interaction – As the hens begin to nest, large numbers of drakes gather on marshes to molt, sometimes traveling many miles from the nesting grounds. Nonbreeding hens may also join this flock. Nesting hens remain with their broods until the juveniles can fly, and generally molt on waters near their nesting grounds.

The drake is a vocal bird with a loud "preep-preep" call. The hen is relatively quiet, but occasionally makes a hurried quack when startled.

Population – Increasing; this bird is less susceptible to drought conditions than most other waterfowl.

Hunting Strategies – Greenwings often challenge hunters by swooping low over decoys, only to rise and fly away without landing. These little ducks are deceptively fast, and often fly in small, tight flocks. Most birds are taken incidentally by hunters seeking other puddle ducks.

Eating Quality – Excellent; the meat is tender and mild-tasting.

Green-winged teal drake

Cinnamon teal drake

Cinnamon Teal
(Anas cyanoptera)

Common Name – Red teal.

Description – This puddle duck is named for the cinnamon color of the drake. In full breeding plumage, the drake has a powder-blue shoulder patch and an iridescent green speculum. The bill is black; the legs and feet, orange. During fall, when drakes are

completing the molt, their colors are not yet fully developed.

The hen, often confused with the hen bluewing, is an overall mottled brown, with a darker brown back and lighter buff undersides. She has a large, powder-blue shoulder patch, a dark gray bill, and dull yellowish legs and feet. Juveniles resemble adult hens, but by early fall the young males begin to develop their reddish adult colors.

Size – Adults measure 14 to 17 inches long and weigh ½ to 1 pound. Drakes are slightly larger than hens.

Migration – Most cinnamon teal breed near Utah's Great Salt Lake, but the breeding range also includes most of the western states, extending into Mexico and slightly into Canada. Like bluewings, cinnamon teal are early migrants, departing the breeding areas

Cinnamon teal hen

in late August and early September. They arrive on the wintering grounds in late November and December.

Most cinnamon teal winter on the marshes and lakes of Mexico, Central and South America, but a few spend the winter in the southwestern United States.

Habitat – Cinnamon teal prefer to breed around marshes and freshwater lakes bordered with emergent vegetation. They also winter on lakes and marshes, including lakes·at high altitude and occasionally on coastal marshes.

Food Habits – Preferred foods of cinnamon teal include the seeds of bulrushes and saltgrass, and the seeds and leaves of pondweed. They also eat mollusks and other aquatic invertebrates.

Breeding – Most birds begin to breed in their first year. After breeding, the hen seeks out a dense stand of grasses or rushes, where she constructs a nest lined with vegetation. She lays about 9 pinkish eggs, which she cushions with her own down. The eggs hatch in about 23 days.

Social Interaction – Cinnamon teal congregate in smaller groups than do most ducks. Migration flocks consist of 10 to 30 birds. The birds quack softly and make a variety of clucking sounds.

Population – Stable; since the 1960s, cinnamon teal numbers in North America have held steady.

Hunting Strategies – Many cinnamon teal are taken incidentally by waterfowlers hunting mallards and pintails over decoys.

Eating Quality – Excellent; like other teal, this bird has mild-tasting meat.

Northern Shoveler

(Anas clypeata)

Common Names – Spoonbill, spoony, neighbor's mallard.

Description – With its unique spoon-shaped bill, this puddle duck is easily identified at close range. The drake is a colorful bird with an iridescent green head, white breast, chestnut flanks, green speculum and large powder-blue shoulder patch. The bill is black.

The hen resembles the hen mallard, but the bill is dull gray to brown. The legs and feet of both sexes are orangish. Juveniles resemble adult hens, but by early fall young males develop the colorful adult plumage.

Size – Adults measure 17 to 20 inches long and weigh 1 to 2 pounds. Drakes are slightly larger than hens.

Migration – Shovelers breed from the prairies of western Minnesota to northwestern Alaska, but most are found in the prairie provinces of Alberta, Saskatchewan and Manitoba. They also breed in the Great Lakes region. These birds are early migrants, beginning the fall migration in early September and reaching the wintering areas by late November. They winter in California, the extreme southern United States, and Mexico.

Habitat – Preferred breeding habit includes shallow freshwater lakes, marshes and seasonally flooded ponds with muddy margins. In the wintering areas, shovelers usually inhabit brackish or saltwater bays and lagoons.

Food Habits – The shoveler eats more small animal life than any other puddle duck. It strains water through its large, spoon-shaped bill to extract plankton and other small organisms, and skims the surface of the mud for insects, mollusks and other invertebrates. It also eats duckweed, pondweeds, wigeon grass and other aquatic plants.

Breeding – Shovelers begin breeding in their first year. With the help of the drake, the hen chooses a

Northern shoveler drake and hen (inset)

nesting site in a shortgrass prairie or hay field, often very close to her previous year's site and usually near water. She constructs a nest of matted vegetation, lining it with her own down. She lays 6 to 13 pale green eggs, which hatch in about 24 days.

Social Interaction – Shovelers usually congregate in pairs or small groups around the edges of small bodies of water. During the migration, they gather in

large groups at stopovers along the route, often mixing with other duck species.

The hen quacks softly, but the drake occasionally makes a hollow-sounding "g'dunk-g'dunk-g'dunk."

Population – Increasing; shovelers are less susceptible to drought than most other ducks, and their numbers have climbed steadily since the 1950s.

Hunting Strategies – Because they often mix with other species, shovelers usually are taken incidentally by waterfowlers hunting for mallards and other ducks. They are rarely targeted intentionally.

Eating Quality – Fair; the meat is very dark and can be rather strong-tasting.

Fulvous Whistling Duck
(Dendrocygna bicolor)

Common Names – Fulvous tree duck, Mexican squealer, pichiguila.

Description – With its long neck and legs, the fulvous whistling duck looks like no other puddle duck found in the continental United States.

In both sexes, the neck and sides of the head are reddish brown; the crown, dark brown. Light streaks separate the dark-brown back from the tawny sides and belly. The bill, legs and feet are blue-gray. Juveniles resemble adult birds, although their plumage is slightly duller.

Size – Adults measure 16 to 18 inches long and weigh 1 to 2 pounds. Drakes are slightly larger than females.

Migration – This duck has one of the widest worldwide distributions of any waterfowl species. Besides North and South America, it is found in India and east Africa. In North America, it breeds in northern Mexico, and in parts of Florida, Louisiana, Texas and California. Birds in the northern part of the range may migrate in late October and November to marshes in the southern part of the range. Southern birds seldom migrate.

Habitat – The preferred habitat is freshwater lakes and marshes, flooded rice fields and coastal saltwater marshes.

Food Habits – Rice is the preferred food, but whistling ducks also eat acorns, grasses and grass seeds. Large flocks often fly into rice fields at sunset.

Breeding – Fulvous whistling ducks mate for life, typically breeding in their first year. Using vegetation, the hen builds a nest a few inches above water, usually in a rice field or fringe of a marsh. She lays about 12 whitish eggs, which hatch in approximately 25 days. The drake helps raise the brood.

Social Interaction – Although generally found in small groups, these ducks may congregate in flocks of up to 100 birds when feeding in rice fields. The fulvous whistling duck is highly vocal in flight. As the name suggests, it has a whistling call, consisting of a distinctive "k-weeoo."

Population – Increasing; numbers have climbed dramatically since the 1960s because of an increase in rice farming.

Hunting Strategies – Most birds taken in the United States are shot incidentally by waterfowlers hunting for other ducks.

Eating Quality – Good; the meat is dark, with a rich, nutty flavor.

Mottled Duck
(Anas fulvigula)

Common Names – Florida mallard, summer duck, Florida duck.

Description – This puddle duck is easily confused with the black duck and hen mallard. But it has a slightly lighter body color than the black duck, and can be distinguished from the hen mallard by the black rather than white borders on the bluish speculum.

Drakes have olive-green bills; hens, orange bills with dark spots. Both sexes have orange legs and feet. Juveniles resemble adults.

Size – Adults measure 17½ to 24 inches long and weigh 2 to 3 pounds. Drakes are slightly larger than hens.

Migration – Most mottled ducks breed in Florida and along the Gulf Coast from Alabama to northern Mexico. Although they do not migrate in the same fashion as other ducks, mottled ducks move inland during September and October to feed in rice fields. They return to coastal marshes in winter.

Habitat – Mottled ducks prefer freshwater marshes and flooded grasslands, but can also be found in brackish coastal marshes and estuaries.

Food Habits – Mottled ducks feed primarily on fish, snails, crayfish and aquatic insects. They also eat rice, wild millet and pondweeds.

Breeding – These birds begin to breed in their first year. The hen often chooses a nesting site very close to where she was hatched. She typically builds a nest on a clump of cordgrass close to water, then lays 9 to 11 eggs, which hatch in about 26 days.

Social Interaction – As hens begin nesting duties, drakes congregate on nearby ponds to molt. When the young are able to fly, the rest of the birds join the molting flock. Mottled ducks utter quacking sounds similar to those made by mallards.

Population – Increasing; expanded rice farming along coastal areas has provided more food and habitat for this duck.

Hunting Strategies – Mottled ducks usually are taken incidentally by hunters seeking mallards or other ducks. They readily respond to mallard calls and decoy spreads.

Eating Quality – Fair; the meat may have a somewhat strong taste.

Canvasback drake (left) and hen (right)

Canvasback
(Aythya valisineria)

Common Name – Can.

Description – This large diving duck is sometimes mistaken for the redhead, but the canvasback's ruddy red head has a longer, straighter profile from the crown to the tip of the bill. The sides and back are whitish gray, and are much lighter than those of the drake redhead. The belly is white; the tail, rump and bib, black.

The hen's body is an overall drab gray, with a sandy brown head. On both sexes, the bill is black and the feet are bluish gray. Juvenile females closely resemble adult hens. Young males have brownish heads and chests until fall, when they develop their adult plumage.

Size – Adults measure 18 to 22 inches long and weigh 2 to 3½ pounds. Drakes are slightly larger than hens.

Migration – Canvasbacks breed from central Alaska through western Canada to Minnesota, and in some of the western states. Most, however, are found in the prairie pothole region. Canvasbacks begin the fall migration in September, stopping along the way on large lakes and rivers, sometimes for several weeks at a time. By January, most birds have reached their wintering grounds.

The birds winter in the Atlantic and Pacific coast states, the Gulf Coast states and Mexico. Smaller wintering concentrations are found around the Great Lakes and in Oklahoma, Arkansas and Arizona.

Habitat – Canvasbacks prefer prairie marshes for nesting. In winter they usually are found on large lakes, and in coastal bays and estuaries.

Food Habits – Canvasbacks have a strong preference for wild celery; in fact, their species name, *valisineria*, is derived from the Latin name for wild celery. But because this aquatic plant has been decimated throughout much of their range, the birds now feed largely on sago pondweed, arrowhead root and bulrush seeds. They also eat mollusks, crustaceans and fish.

Breeding – These birds will breed in their first year if there is plenty of water and cover on the breeding grounds. If conditions are dry, they usually wait until their second year.

Canvasbacks usually nest in dense emergent vegetation, primarily cattails and bulrushes, along the fringes of marshes. The hen uses the vegetation to build a large, bulky nest, then lays a clutch of about 8 greenish eggs, which hatch in 23 to 25 days. Redhead hens sometimes lay their eggs in canvasback nests, causing the canvasback hen to lay fewer eggs.

Social Interaction – Shortly after nesting begins, drakes leave the hens to congregate on large, open-water marshes, where they may be joined by non-nesting females. For the midsummer molt, these flocks sometimes move to the open waters of large lakes, forming *rafts* of hundreds of birds.

Neither the hen nor the drake is particularly vocal. The drake makes a low croak; the hen, a sharp "krrr" or quack.

Population – Rising, but still below the long-term average. During the drought of the 1980s, numbers dropped low enough that the hunting season was closed for several years. Rising water levels and wild celery restoration efforts have improved the population enough to warrant the reopening of the season.

Hunting Strategies – You can lure canvasbacks with a simple decoy pattern often used for diving ducks: set one or more lines of decoys, and use a diver call to lead the birds into shotgun range of your blind. These birds are the among the fastest ducks, making them difficult to pass-shoot.

Eating Quality – Excellent; in the days of market hunting, these mild-tasting ducks drew top price.

Redhead drake

Redhead
(Aythya americana)

Common Name – Pochard.

Description – The drake of this popular diving duck resembles the canvasback drake. It has a reddish head, black bib and rump, and white belly, but it is slightly smaller with a more rounded forehead profile, and a darker back and sides. The bill is blue-gray, with a black tip.

The hen has a reddish brown head, neck and breast, drab brown back and sides, and white undersides. The pattern on her bill is slightly less conspicuous than on the male. Both sexes have gray legs and feet.

Juveniles resemble hens until fall, when the young males begin to develop the brilliant adult plumage.

Size – Adults measure 18 to 22 inches long and weigh 1½ to 3 pounds. Drakes are slightly larger than hens.

Migration – Redheads nest primarily in the prairie pothole region, but significant numbers also breed in the area around the Great Salt Lake. Smaller breeding populations are found in other western states, around the Great Lakes, in Alaska and Minnesota. Redheads depart their breeding grounds in September and October and reach their wintering areas by November and December. The birds winter across most of the South, in the Ozarks, in nearly all of the

44

Redhead hen

western states, along the Atlantic seaboard, and throughout most of Mexico.

Habitat – Redheads nest on prairie marshes and freshwater lakes fringed with emergent vegetation. They winter mostly on lakes and reservoirs, and on tidal bays and estuaries.

Food Habits – Redheads consume more plant material than most diving ducks. They tend to feed in shallow waters, where they seek out pondweeds, coontail, wild celery, muskgrass, bulrushes and duckweed.

Breeding – Redheads hatched early in the season often breed in their first year, but those hatched late generally do not breed until their second year. They prefer nesting sites in emergent vegetation in shallow water, but may lay their eggs in the nests of other ducks.

The hen uses vegetation to weave a bowl-shaped nest, which is lined with down and anchored to

cattails or bulrushes. She lays 10 to 12 buff-colored eggs, which hatch in 24 to 28 days.

Social Interaction – These birds often flock together with canvasbacks and scaup, especially on the wintering grounds. The drake makes distinctive "whee-ough" and rolling "rrrrr" sounds; the hen, sharp quacking sounds.

Population – Increasing; improvement in water conditions across the prairie pothole region has caused the bird's numbers to rise steadily since the early 1990s.

Hunting Strategies – Most birds are taken incidentally by waterfowlers hunting scaup late in the season. Redheads are easily lured by scaup decoy lines.

Eating Quality – Excellent; the meat is milder in taste than that of many diving ducks.

Lesser scaup drake and hen (inset)

Lesser Scaup

(Aythya affinis)

Common Name – Bluebill.

Description – This diving duck closely resembles its slightly larger cousin, the greater scaup. The drake's dark head has a purple sheen, however, in contrast to the greenish sheen on the greater scaup. The bill, for which the bird receives its common name, is blue-gray with a black tip. The drake's neck, chest and rump are black; the sides and undersides, white. The back is mottled with black and white.

The hen is dark brown overall; the head and breast are slightly darker than the sides and back. The undersides are whitish. A white ring circles the base of the bill. Both sexes have blue-gray legs and feet, and a long white speculum. Juveniles resemble adult hens.

Size – Adults measure 15 to 18 inches long and weigh 1 to 2½ pounds. Drakes are slightly larger than hens.

Migration – These birds breed in the prairie pothole region, parts of the Northwest, western Canada and most of Alaska. The fall migration begins in September, and most birds arrive on their wintering areas between October and December. The birds winter in most of the coastal states and Mexico.

Habitat – Lesser scaup nest near prairie marshes, and shallow ponds and lakes fringed with emergent vegetation. They winter on coastal bays and estuaries, and on large freshwater lakes.

Food Habits – Primary foods include aquatic invertebrates, such as clams and snails, but lesser scaup also eat smartweed and aquatic plants, including wild celery, wigeon grass and bulrushes.

Breeding – The birds seldom breed before their second year. Unlike most diving ducks, the hen builds her nest in an upland area, using grasses, sedges and other vegetation. She lays about 9 dark olive eggs, which hatch in approximately 25 days.

Social Interaction – Just before the molt, these ducks gather in huge flocks and fly to lakes in forested areas. They often winter with greater scaup. Drakes utter soft whistling notes; hens, low growling sounds.

Population – Because all scaup are counted together in waterfowl surveys, numbers are difficult to determine. Biologists believe the population may be declining slightly. Lesser scaup have not responded to improving water levels in the prairie pothole region as well as most other ducks.

Hunting Strategies – The most common technique is to use a long line of decoys and a diver call to lead the birds to within shooting range of your blind.

Eating Quality – Good; the dark meat is not as strong as that of many diving ducks.

Greater scaup drake and hen (inset)

Greater Scaup
(Aythya marila)

Common Names – Bluebill, broadbill.

Description – This diving duck is nearly identical to the lesser scaup, but is slightly larger. Like the drake lesser, the drake greater scaup has a black chest and rump, white sides and undersides, and a back mottled with black and white. But his head has a greenish sheen rather than a purple hue.

The hen's overall body color is dark brown with whitish undersides. A white ring circles the base of the bill. Both sexes have blue-gray legs and feet, a blue-gray bill with a black tip, and a white speculum. Juveniles resemble adult hens.

Size – Adults measure 15½ to 20 inches long and weigh 1½ to 3 pounds. Drakes are slightly larger than hens.

Migration – Greater scaup breed in most of Alaska and the Yukon, and parts of northern Canada. They begin the fall migration in September, reaching the wintering grounds in October. These ducks winter along most of the Atlantic, Pacific and Gulf coasts, and on the lower Great Lakes.

Habitat – Greater scaup nest on tundra lakes and ponds. They winter on large lakes, and in coastal bays and estuaries.

Food Habits – Clams are the food of choice for these diving ducks, but they also feed on aquatic plants, including pondweeds, wild celery and sea lettuce.

Breeding – Greater scaup rarely breed before their second year. The hen chooses a nesting site close to water on lowland tundra – usually on an elevated mound with a good view of the surrounding area – where she uses grasses to build a bowl-shaped nest. She may lay her eggs in the nest of another duck. The average clutch consists of 9 olive-colored eggs, which hatch in 23 to 28 days.

Social Interaction – Highly social, greater scaup often gather in large rafts while on their wintering grounds. Both sexes make soft croaking sounds; the drake also coos and whistles.

Population – Numbers are difficult to estimate because flocks often combine with those of lesser scaup, but most biologists believe the population is stable.

Hunting Strategies – Greater scaup are hunted in the same way as lessers – by using diver calls and setting long lines of decoys to draw birds to your blind.

Eating Quality – Good; identical to that of the lesser scaup.

Ring-necked duck drake (left) and hen (right)

Ring-Necked Duck

(Aythya collaris)

Common Names –
Ringneck, ring-billed duck,
ringbill, blackjack.

Description – This diving
duck's name is somewhat
misleading, because the
chestnut ring around the
drake's neck is visible only
at close range.

The drake has a black head
with a purple-blue sheen.
The back and bib are black; the sides, grayish white;

the belly, white. The slate-gray bill is edged with
white and has a distinctive white ring near the tip,
accounting for its common name – ringbill.

The hen has tan sides, a brown back and white belly.
Her bill ring is less pronounced than on the drake.
Juveniles resemble adult hens, though the young
males have a more distinctive bill ring.

Size – Adults measure 16 to 18 inches long and
weigh 1 to 2 pounds. Drakes are slightly larger
than hens.

Migration – Ring-necked ducks breed across much
of Canada, but are most concentrated in Alberta,
Saskatchewan and Manitoba. Breeding populations
are also found in Alaska, the Pacific Northwest, the
Rocky Mountain states, the Great Lakes region and
upper New England.

The fall migration begins in September, with most
birds reaching wintering areas between October and
December. Most ringnecks winter in the southern

48

United States and Mexico, but wintering birds are found in nearly all coastal states.

Habitat – Ringnecks nest on small lakes and marshes in wooded areas, and occasionally can be found on small rivers. In winter, the birds frequent large freshwater lakes, and may seek out brackish waters in coastal estuaries. They are seldom found in salt water.

Food Habits – Favorite foods include the leaves and seeds of pondweeds, duckweed, coontail and a variety of other aquatic plants. Although they are diving ducks, ringnecks prefer water just a few feet deep, feeding in seasonal pools, shallow ponds and marshes.

Breeding – Unlike many diving ducks, ringnecks generally breed in their first year. Typically, the hen chooses a nesting site on a pond in a wooded area, often near an island, where she builds her nest on a small cluster of floating vegetation. She lays 8 or 9 olive eggs, which hatch in 25 to 29 days. The drake sometimes stays with the hen through incubation.

Social Interaction – These birds usually fly in small flocks of no more than a few dozen birds. On the wintering grounds, they may form larger flocks, usually remaining near shore.

The drake makes a low whistling note, and the hen utters a gentle rolling "rrrr."

Population – Increasing; ringneck numbers have climbed slowly but steadily since the 1950s, because their breeding areas are not affected by drought as much as those of other ducks.

Hunting Strategies – Most ring-necked ducks are taken incidentally by waterfowlers hunting other divers, but a few dedicated hunters intentionally seek these birds, setting out lines of decoys and using diver calls.

Eating Quality – Good; one of the milder-tasting diving ducks.

Common goldeneye drake and hen (inset)

Common Goldeneye
(Bucephala clangula)

Common Name – Whistler.

Description – This diving duck's common name is derived from the distinctive whistling sound made by its wings. Like many other divers, it has a yellowish gold eye. The drake has a black head with a greenish sheen, a round white spot in front of the eye, and a black

bill. A row of black and white streaked feathers separates the white chest and undersides from the black rump and back.

The hen's head is dark brown, with no facial spot. The sides and back are gray; the belly, white. Her bill is dark, with a yellowish tip. Both sexes have yellowish legs and feet. Juveniles resemble adult females.

Size – Adults measure 16 to 20 inches long and weigh 1½ to 3⅓ pounds. Drakes are slightly larger than hens.

Migration – Common goldeneyes breed across most of Canada, in much of Alaska, and in parts of the extreme northern continental United States. This hardy bird, one of the last ducks to migrate, remains in the breeding range until forced south by freezing waters. By late November, most birds have reached their wintering areas. Common goldeneyes winter throughout the United States and along the Pacific coast of Alaska and Canada.

Habitat – Common goldeneyes nest around slow-moving rivers and lakes in wooded areas. They winter on large freshwater lakes, and on coastal bays and estuaries.

Food Habits – Most of the diet consists of aquatic invertebrates and fish. Goldeneyes also eat aquatic plants, including wild celery, and the seeds of bulrushes, pondweeds and water lily.

Breeding – These birds rarely mate before their second year. The hen typically nests in a tree cavity or man-made nest box. The hen lays about 9 greenish blue eggs, which hatch in approximately 30 days. Occasionally, the hen lays her eggs in the nest of another duck.

Social Interaction – Goldeneyes are usually found in tight groups numbering 30 birds or less, and rarely mix with other species. Other than their wing noise, goldeneyes are relatively quiet. The drake sometimes makes a "jeee-ep" call; the hen, low guttural quacks.

Population – Stable; weather conditions have little effect on these cavity-nesting birds.

Hunting Strategies – Common goldeneyes are usually hunted over long points of land on big water, either by leading the birds in with strings of decoys or by pass-shooting.

Eating Quality – Fair; the meat is dark and can be very strong.

Barrow's goldeneye drake (left) and hen (right)

Barrow's Goldeneye
(Bucephala islandica)

Common Names – Whistler, Rocky Mountain whistler.

Description – Like the common goldeneye, this diving duck produces loud whistling noises in flight.

The white spot in front of the drake's eye is crescent-shaped rather than round, as on the common goldeneye, and his head has a purplish rather than greenish sheen. The black back, which has rows of white spots, extends farther down the sides than on the common goldeneye. The undersides are white, and the bill is black.

The hen's back and sides are gray; the belly, white. Her brown head is darker than the common goldeneye's. The bill is orange-yellow, with a black base and tip. Both sexes have yellowish legs and feet. Juveniles resemble adult hens.

Size – Adults measure 16 to 20 inches long and weigh 1 to 2½ pounds. Drakes are slightly larger than hens.

Migration – The birds breed mainly in mountainous areas from Oregon and western Wyoming to central Alaska, with smaller numbers breeding in northern Labrador and Quebec. Most birds leave the breeding grounds by early October, arriving on the wintering grounds from late October to early November. Drakes usually migrate before the hens. The birds winter along the Pacific coast from Alaska to central California, along most of the Atlantic coast of Canada, and on the lower Colorado River. Birds in mountainous regions do not migrate.

Habitat – Barrow's goldeneyes breed on lakes and rivers in wooded areas, often at high elevation. In the eastern part of the range, they breed on tundra. The birds winter on coastal bays and estuaries, or on any open waters in mountainous regions.

Food Habits – The diet consists mainly of aquatic insects, mollusks and fish. The birds also feed on aquatic plants, especially sago pondweed.

Breeding – Most birds begin breeding in their second year. The hen prefers to nest in a tree cavity or man-made nest box lined with her own down, but also may nest in a hole in the ground or among rocks. Repeat nesters often return to their previous nesting sites. The hen lays about 9 whitish green eggs, which hatch in approximately 33 days.

Social Interaction – These birds congregate in groups even smaller than those of the common goldeneye. After leaving their mates, drakes join together in molting flocks. Hens remain with the brood until the young can fly, then form their own molting flock. Though these ducks are relatively silent, the drake sometimes utters a softly grunted "ka-KAA" sound.

Population – Stable; these cavity-nesting ducks have consistent breeding success.

Hunting Strategies – Most Barrow's goldeneyes are taken incidentally by hunters seeking other diving duck species.

Eating Quality – Fair; the meat is similar in taste to that of the common goldeneye.

Bufflehead
(Bucephala albeola)

Common Names –
Butterball, dipper.

Description – This small
diving duck gets the name
"butterball" from its chubby
shape. The drake's head is
black with a green and purple
sheen, and has a white
wedge-shaped patch behind
the eye. The back is black;
the sides and belly, white.
The bill is blue-gray; the feet and legs, pinkish.

The hen's head is dark brown with a small white
patch behind the eye. The back is dark brown; the
sides, grayish; the belly, white. The legs and feet are
grayish; the bill, a darker gray. Juveniles resemble
adult hens, though they lack the white patch.

Size – Adults measure 13 to 16 inches long and weigh
¾ to 1½ pounds. Drakes are slightly larger than hens.

Migration – Buffleheads breed across much of the
Alaskan interior, throughout most of Canada, and in
the northern Rockies and Cascades of the continental
United States. The fall migration begins in mid-October,
with the birds arriving on wintering areas in November
and December. Birds winter over most of the continental United States, except for the north central states, and
in northern Mexico.

Habitat – These birds breed on small lakes, ponds
and slow-moving rivers in wooded areas. They winter
on coastal bays and estuaries, and on large lakes and
rivers.

Food Habits – The diet consists mostly of fish and
aquatic invertebrates, but the birds also feed on aquatic plants.

Breeding – Most birds begin breeding in their second
year. They nest in holes in trees near water, often
holes made by flickers in aspen trees. The hen lays
about 9 creamy buff eggs, which hatch in approximately 30 days.

Social Interaction – Buffleheads congregate in small
groups, and occasionally mix with other diving ducks.
Drakes gather on lakes to molt, where they are joined
by nonbreeding hens. Hens stay with their broods
until the young can fly; then all the birds join the
molting flock. Although they are fairly quiet birds,
the drake makes squeaky whistles and guttural notes;
the hen, soft quacks.

Population – Stable; weather and predators have relatively little effect on these cavity-nesting ducks.

Hunting Strategies – Most birds are taken incidentally by hunters pursuing other divers.

Eating Quality – Fair; the dark meat can be
strong-tasting.

Bufflehead hen (left) and drake (right)

Ruddy Duck
(Oxyura jamaicensis)

Common Names – Bull-necked teal, butterball.

Description – This small, chunky diver has a broad bill, gray legs and feet, and unusually stiff tail feathers. These birds swim very low in the water and, when threatened, escape by sinking slowly out of sight. The drake's plumage varies seasonally. In summer, he has a chestnut body and neck, a black crown, large white cheek patches, and a pale blue bill. In fall and winter, his color fades to resemble that of the hen, and his bill turns black. He retains the large white cheek patches, however.

The hen is dusky brown overall, with a darker back, chest and crown, and buff-colored undersides. The whitish cheeks are streaked with brown, and the bill is dull blackish blue. Juveniles resemble adult hens.

Size – Adults measure 14½ to 16 inches long and weigh ½ to 1½ pounds. Drakes are slightly larger than hens.

Migration – The birds breed in most of the western states, in the Great Lakes region, and in much of western Canada. The fall migration begins in September, and by December most birds reach wintering areas in the southern United States, the Atlantic and Pacific coastal states, and Mexico.

Habitat – The birds breed on marshes and shallow, weedy lakes. They winter on shallow coastal bays and estuaries, as well as on freshwater marshes.

Food Habits – The diet consists mostly of plants, including pondweeds, wigeon grass and bulrush seeds, but ruddy ducks also eat larval aquatic insects. These divers prefer shallow water, usually feeding at depths of 2 to 10 feet.

Breeding – Most birds do not mate until their second year. The hen typically builds a floating nest on dense vegetation over shallow water, but she may lay her eggs in the nest of another duck. The average clutch consists of 8 cream-colored eggs, which hatch in about 25 days.

Social Interaction – On the wintering grounds, ruddy ducks form large rafts. These birds are generally silent.

Population – Stable; these birds have a high rate of nesting success, probably because their shallow-water nesting sites are safe from most predators.

Hunting Strategies – Most birds are taken incidentally by hunters pursuing other species.

Eating Quality – Good; this plant-eating diver has a milder taste than many diving ducks.

Ruddy duck drake and hen (inset)

Common merganser drake and hens (inset)

Common Merganser
(Mergus merganser)

Common Names – American merganser, saw-bill, fish duck, goosander.

Description – This large bird has the pointed bill characteristic of all mergansers. The drake has a dark green head with no crest, a black back, and white sides and belly.

The hen's crested head is brown; the back, chest and sides are gray; the belly, white. Both sexes have red bills and feet. Juveniles resemble adult hens.

Size – Drakes measure 23 to 27 inches long and weigh 2 to 4½ pounds; hens, 21 to 26 inches long and 2 to 3 pounds.

Migration – These birds breed in several western and Rocky Mountain states, in the Great Lakes region, and in a wide band extending across Canada and into Alaska.

Because it readily copes with cold temperatures, the common merganser is one of the last waterfowl to fly south in the fall. Moving gradually as ice forms on rivers and lakes, most birds reach their wintering grounds by November and December. The wintering range includes most of the continental United States, the Pacific coast of Canada and Alaska, and a small portion of northern Mexico.

Habitat – Common mergansers nest near ponds and rivers in wooded areas. They winter on larger lakes and rivers, and occasionally on coastal bays.

Food Habits – Like most mergansers, this species feeds primarily on small fish, such as minnows, and has been known to eat salmon, trout and other game fish.

Breeding – Mergansers generally do not breed until their second year. The hen prefers to nest in a tree cavity, but if no such site is available, she will construct a ground nest in a rock crevice or small depression close to water. Most clutches consist of 10 or 11 cream-colored eggs, which hatch in about 30 days. Two hens sometimes share a single nest and raise the combined brood together.

Social Interaction – Young birds typically assemble in nonbreeding flocks until they reach sexual maturity. Although they usually congregate in groups of no more than a dozen birds, common mergansers may gather in larger flocks when diving for fish. Common mergansers sometimes make hoarse croaks.

Population – Stable; like other cavity nesters, these birds have a high rate of nesting success.

Hunting Strategies – Most birds are taken incidentally by hunters seeking other diving ducks, but these strikingly beautiful birds are sometimes sought by collectors for taxidermy purposes.

Eating Quality – Poor; the meat has a distinctly fishy flavor.

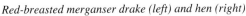

Red-breasted merganser drake (left) and hen (right)

Red-Breasted Merganser

(Mergus serrator)

Common Names – Sawbill, fish duck.

Description – The distinctive drake has a crested green head, a reddish brown chest, a black back, and a white belly.

The hen has a reddish brown head with a less pronounced crest. The back and sides are gray; the belly, white. Both sexes have red feet and narrow red bills. Juveniles resemble adult hens.

Size – Adults measure 18 to 23 inches long and weigh 1½ to 3 pounds. Drakes are slightly larger than hens.

Migration – Red-breasted mergansers have a wide breeding range that stretches from Newfoundland to western Alaska. In the United States, the birds breed in Maine and the Great Lakes region. Most birds begin the fall migration in November and reach wintering areas by the end of December. The wintering range includes the coastal areas of the United States, Canada, and western Mexico, as well as the Great Lakes region.

Habitat – Red-breasted mergansers nest around lakes in wooded areas and around tundra ponds. They winter on coastal bays and estuaries, and on large freshwater lakes.

Food Habits – The diet includes a variety of fish, such as minnows, sticklebacks, suckers, sunfish and salmon. The birds also feed on crustaceans.

Breeding – Red-breasted mergansers nest in loose colonies. They begin to breed when they are two years old. Unlike the other mergansers, redbreasts nest on the ground-often on islands, where there are few predators. The nest is usually among rocks, under dense bushes, or in thick grass. The hen builds a nest using grasses and her own down. She lays about 8 buff-colored eggs, which hatch in approximately 30 days.

Social Interaction – The birds often group together when feeding on fish. Migration flocks are usually small, consisting of no more than 15 birds.

Although the birds are relatively silent, they occasionally make hoarse croaks.

Population – Stable; their habit of nesting on islands ensures a high rate of nesting success.

Hunting Strategies – Most birds are taken incidentally by waterfowlers hunting for other species.

Eating Quality – Poor; the breast meat is dark and has a fishy taste.

Hooded merganser drake and hen (inset)

Hooded Merganser
(Lophodytes cucullatus)

Common Names – Fish duck, sawbill.

Description – The drake is a handsome bird, with a pronounced fan-shaped, black-and-white crest. The back is black with white stripes. The sides are brownish; the breast and belly, white. The legs and feet are brownish yellow; the bill, black.

The hen has a reddish brown crested head and a dark back. The belly is white; the sides, gray. The bill is blackish on top and yellowish below. The legs and feet are yellowish gray. Both sexes have white leading edges on the wings. Juvenile males do not develop their colorful adult plumage until their second winter. Juvenile females resemble adult hens, but have less pronounced crests.

Size – Adults measure 16 to 19 inches long and weigh 1¼ to 2 pounds. Drakes are slightly larger than hens.

Migration – In the West, the breeding range extends from the Alaskan panhandle south into the mountains of Washington, Oregon, Idaho and Montana. The eastern breeding range includes southern Canada and much of the eastern United States, with the largest concentration found in the Great Lakes region. The fall migration begins in October, with most birds reaching their wintering areas by November and December. They winter in the southeastern United States, along the Atlantic seaboard as far north as Cape Cod, and along the Pacific coast from the Alaskan panhandle to the Baja Peninsula.

Habitat – Hooded mergansers nest near slow-moving rivers, small ponds and lakes in wooded areas. They winter on similar types of waters, as well as in coastal marshes, bays and estuaries.

Food Habits – The diet consists mostly of crustaceans, frogs, aquatic insects and fish. These birds usually feed near shore, and eat less fish than the other merganser species.

Breeding – Most birds begin to breed as two-year-olds. The hen typically nests in a down-lined tree cavity near water, but will also nest in man-made nest boxes. Hens have been known to lay their eggs in another duck's nest. The average clutch consists of 10 white eggs, which hatch in about 32 days.

Social Interaction – These birds rarely mingle with other species, preferring to spend their time in small groups of no more than 12 birds. Normally silent, they may utter coarse grunts and croaks.

Population – Stable; like most cavity nesters, hooded mergansers have a high rate of nesting success.

Hunting Strategies – Most birds are taken incidentally by waterfowlers hunting other species.

Eating Quality – Poor; the meat is dark and has a strong fishy flavor.

White-Winged Scoter
(Melanitta fusca)

Common Names – Sea coot, whitewing, velvet scoter.

Description – This sea duck is named for its white speculum. The drake has all-black plumage, except for the speculum and a small white crescent around the eye. The orange-yellow bill has a dark knob at the base, and a reddish tip. The legs and feet are reddish orange.

The hen's overall color is slightly lighter than the drake's, and her speculum is smaller. She has tannish patches on the cheeks, and a grayish bill with no knob. The legs and feet are grayish yellow to dull orange. Juveniles resemble adult hens, though the immature male has mottled white undersides.

Size – Drakes measure 21 to 23 inches long and weigh 3 to 4 pounds; hens, 19 to 22 inches and 2 to 3 pounds.

Migration – Whitewings breed across much of the Alaskan interior and western Canada. The fall migration begins from September to mid-October, with most birds arriving on wintering areas in December and January. Whitewings complete the migration later than any other species of scoter.

In the West, whitewings winter along the Pacific coast from southern Alaska into the Baja Peninsula. In the East, they winter in the Great Lakes region, along most of the Atlantic coast, and along the Gulf Coast from Texas to the Florida panhandle.

Habitat – These birds nest primarily around lakes and ponds surrounded by sparse woods. They winter on the open ocean, in large coastal bays and on large freshwater lakes.

Food Habits – White-winged scoters eat mussels, crabs, crayfish and barnacles. They may dive to depths up to 90 feet while feeding.

White-winged scoter drake and hen (inset)

Breeding – Most birds first breed in their second or third year. The hen usually selects a nesting site near water, but occasionally can be found nesting hundreds of yards away. She typically builds a nest in a ground hollow, lining it with down and dead vegetation. Whitewings have also been known to use man-made nest boxes. The hen lays about 9 buff-colored eggs, which hatch in approximately 28 days.

Social Interaction – These sea ducks form very large groups during the annual molt and while on their wintering grounds. They often mix with other scoter species. Normally silent, the drake sometimes makes whistling calls; the hen, a raspy "karrr."

Population – Stable; whitewings are the most numerous of the scoter species, and have the largest breeding range.

Hunting Strategies – Hunt whitewings in traditional sea duck fashion, by stringing long lines of decoys into open water to draw the birds into shooting range. Decoys may consist of nothing more than black jugs.

Eating Quality – Poor; the meat is very dark and usually strong-tasting.

Surf Scoter

(Melanitta perspicillata)

Common Names – Sea coot, coot, skunkhead, skunk duck.

Description – This sea duck is called the surf scoter because it feeds along the surf line. The drake is black except for white patches on the forehead and back of the neck. His colorful bill is red, white, yellow and black, with a noticeable hump in the middle.

The hen is grayish brown overall, with a white belly, a small white patch below the eye and a large, grayish black bill. Both sexes have orange legs and feet. Juveniles resemble adult hens.

Size – Adults measure 17 to 21 inches long and weigh 1½ to 2½ pounds. Drakes are slightly larger than hens.

Migration – These birds breed in Alaska and in a wide band across northern Canada. The fall migration begins in late September to early October, and by December most birds have arrived on their wintering grounds. Surf scoters winter along the Pacific coast from Alaska into the Baja Peninsula, along most of the Atlantic coast, in the Great Lakes region, and along a small stretch of the Gulf Coast from the Florida panhandle to Mississippi.

Habitat – These birds nest around rivers, lakes and ponds in sparsely wooded areas. They winter on the open ocean, in large coastal bays and on large freshwater lakes.

Food Habits – The diet consists mostly of mollusks, crustaceans and aquatic insects. The birds also eat aquatic plants, including wigeon grass, pondweeds and eelgrass.

Breeding – Surf scoters begin breeding in their second year. The hen builds a down-lined nest in marsh vegetation near a river, pond or lake, or under a bush far from water. She lays 5 to 7 pinkish white eggs, which hatch in about 30 days.

Social Interaction – For the annual molt, these ducks gather by the thousands along the coasts of Labrador and Alaska, often mixing with other scoter species. Surf scoters are normally silent, but may make low croaks.

Population – Numbers are difficult to determine because all scoter species are counted together in waterfowl surveys, but most biologists believe the population is stable.

Hunting Strategies – These birds are hunted with the same techniques used for whitewings.

Eating Quality – Poor; the meat is very strong-tasting.

Surf scoter drake and hen (inset)

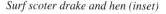

Black Scoter
(Melanitta nigra)

Common Names – Common scoter, American scoter, black coot, sea coot, black duck.

Description – This sea duck is named for the pure black plumage of the drake. The drake's bill is also black, except for the prominent bright yellow knob.

The hen is a mottled brown, with a darker cap and lighter cheeks and throat. Her black bill has no knob. Both sexes have dark gray legs and feet. Juveniles resemble adult hens, but the young male's belly is slightly lighter and is a mottled white.

Size – Adults measure 17 to 21 inches long and weigh 2 to 3 pounds. Drakes are slightly larger than hens.

Migration – The breeding range includes portions of western and central Alaska, and isolated pockets in Newfoundland, Quebec and the Northwest Territories. The fall migration begins in late September, with most birds arriving on the wintering grounds in December. Black scoters winter on the Pacific coast from southern Alaska to California, along most of the Atlantic coast, in the Great Lakes region, and on the Gulf Coast from Texas to the Florida panhandle.

Habitat – During the breeding season, black scoters prefer ponds and lakes in tundra or in wooded country. In winter, they can be found on coastal bays and large freshwater lakes.

Food Habits – Black scoters eat mostly mollusks, such as blue mussels and barnacles, but they also feed on crustaceans and other aquatic invertebrates. Aquatic plants, such as pondweeds and wigeon grass, make up a small portion of the diet.

Breeding – Black scoters seldom breed before age two. The hen typically chooses a site in tundra grass very close to water, where she uses down and dead grasses to construct a well-hidden nest. She lays 5 to 8 buff-colored eggs, which hatch in about 28 days.

Social Interaction – Black scoters congregate in huge flocks along the coasts of Labrador and Alaska, often mingling with the other species of scoter. They make a musical "cour-loo" whistle.

Population – Stable; numbers are lower than for the other scoter species, but biologists believe the population is steady.

Hunting Strategies – Black scoters are hunted with the same methods described for white-winged scoters.

Eating Quality – Poor; the dark meat has a very strong taste.

Black scoter drake and hen (inset)

Common eider hen (left) and drake (right)

Common Eider
(Somateria mollissima)

Common Name – American eider.

Description – This sea duck is the largest North American duck. It has a long, sloping bill that gives the head a distinctive wedge shape.

The drake has a white neck, breast and back, with black flanks and undersides. The head is white with an olive nape, and a white-streaked black crown. The bill is yellowish to olive, with a gray tip.

The hen is tan, mottled with black, and has a grayish bill. Both sexes have grayish legs and feet. Juveniles resemble adult hens.

Size – Drakes measure 22½ to 26½ inches long and weigh 4 to 6½ pounds; hens, 21 to 25 inches long and 3 to 6 pounds.

Migration – Most common eiders breed near the coastlines of Alaska, the Canadian Arctic and Hudson Bay, and in scattered areas of eastern Canada. The fall migration begins in mid-September, with birds arriving on the wintering grounds from mid-October to December. They winter on the coastal waters of Alaska and eastern Canada.

Habitat – Most common eiders nest on tundra and rocky shoreline areas. They winter on the open sea, usually out of sight of land.

Food Habits – These sea ducks eat mostly mollusks, crustaceans and fish. They generally feed in waters 4 to 10 feet deep, but may dive as deep as 60 feet.

Breeding – Most birds do not breed until their third year. Hens typically form loose nesting colonies. A hen typically chooses a sheltered nesting site along a rocky shoreline, where she uses grasses and her own down to build a nest. The drake stands guard while the hen lays 3 or 4 buff-olive eggs, but leaves when she begins incubation, which lasts 26 to 28 days.

Social Interaction – When feeding on a plentiful food source, common eiders may gather in large rafts. The hen makes quacking noises; the drake, an "ahOOoo" call.

Population – Stable; because eiderdown collected from nests is highly valued for clothing, eider nesting sites are carefully guarded in many areas.

Hunting Strategies – These colorful birds are prized by waterfowlers, but are difficult to hunt because they often are found far from shore. The standard technique is to anchor a seaworthy boat well offshore, and surround it with decoys.

Eating Quality – Poor; the meat is dark and usually has a fishy taste.

King eider hen (left) and drake (right)

King Eider
(Somateria spectabilis)

Common Name – Eider.

Description – The drake of this sea duck species is known for its unique, colorful head. A s*hield* of orange and black feathers surrounds the top of the bill. The crown and back of the head are blue-gray; the cheeks, light green. The neck and breast are creamy white, and the rest of the body is black, except for small patches of white on the flanks and on the tops of the wings. Two stiff feathers project from the back. The legs and feet are yellowish orange.

The hen is brown, marked with black crescents, and the olive-gray bill has no shield. The legs and feet are grayish. Juveniles resemble adult hens, but by fall young males begin to show the distinctive forehead.

Size – Adults measure 18 to 25 inches long and weigh 2¾ to 4¼ pounds. Drakes are slightly larger than hens.

Migration – King eiders breed near coastal areas north of the Arctic Circle and along the shores of Hudson Bay. The fall migration begins in July and August, with drakes leaving slightly before the hens. The birds arrive on the wintering grounds from mid-September to December. They winter along the Pacific coast of Alaska and along the Atlantic coast from Virginia to Labrador.

Habitat – King eiders nest on tundra habitat near water. They winter along rocky coastal shorelines, sometimes well out to sea.

Food Habits – These birds eat mostly invertebrates, and are extraordinary divers – they have been observed feeding at depths as great as 180 feet.

Breeding – Most birds begin to breed in their second or third year. Unlike common eiders, kings prefer isolation when nesting. The hen chooses a dry tundra slope, usually overlooking a pool or lake, and sometimes on an island. She creates a down-lined depression, then lays 4 or 5 olive-colored eggs, which hatch in 23 or 24 days.

Social Interaction – As the hens begin incubation, drakes congregate on traditional molting grounds, forming groups that may number in the tens of thousands. The birds make low croaking noises.

Population – Numbers are difficult to determine due to the remoteness of the bird's breeding range, but biologists believe the population is stable.

Hunting Strategies – Its dramatic plumage makes this bird a favorite among bird collectors and a popular trophy duck among many waterfowlers. Hunt them with the same techniques used for common eider.

Eating Quality – Poor; the meat is dark and strong-flavored.

Oldsquaw drake and hen (inset)

Oldsquaw
(Clangula hyemalis)

Common Names – Sea pintail, cockertail, long-tailed duck.

Description – This sea duck has four distinct plumages occurring in different seasons, making identification very difficult. During the hunting season, the drake's back is dark brown, with gray shoulders, and the flanks and neck are white. The white head has tan cheek patches and a dark brown spot at the rear. The black bill has a pink band. The dark brown tail is as long as that of the pintail. Although the overall coloration is darker in the other phases, the long tail is distinctive.

The hen is duller, and her seasonal color shift is less dramatic. The body and wings are mottled with light and dark brown, and the belly is white. In winter, the head has equal amounts of patchy white and brown plumage, but in summer, it is mostly dark. The tail is much shorter than the drake's, and the bill is gray. Both sexes have gray legs and feet. Juveniles resemble adult hens, but by fall young males begin to show adult plumage.

Size – Drakes measure 19 to 23 inches long and weigh 2 to 2½ pounds; hens, 15 to 17 inches and 1½ to 2 pounds.

Migration – This bird breeds across northern Alaska and the Canadian Arctic, and around Hudson Bay. Usually flying at night, oldsquaws begin the fall migration in early September, completing the journey by November or December. They winter on the Pacific coast from western Alaska to California, along most of the Atlantic coast, in the Great Lakes region, and along the Gulf Coast from Louisiana to the Florida panhandle.

Habitat – During the nesting season, oldsquaws can be found on tundra, usually near lakes or ponds, and along rocky coastlines. They winter on coastal bays and large inland lakes.

Food Habits – Crustaceans, mollusks, fish and insect larvae comprise most of the bird's diet. Oldsquaws regularly feed at depths of 20 to 30 feet, and have been known to dive as deep as 200.

Breeding – Oldsquaws begin breeding in their second year. The hen typically chooses a nesting site close to the water's edge, along the seacoast or a freshwater lake or pond. In a sheltered spot, she constructs a bowl-shaped nest using grasses and down, then lays about 7 cream-colored eggs, which hatch in approximately 26 days.

Social Interaction – Oldsquaws spend much of their time at sea, where they form large rafts. Hens often gather in nesting colonies during the breeding season. Considered one of the most vocal of all ducks, oldsquaws make a variety of yodeling, clucking and growling sounds.

Population – Although they are not often seen in North America, oldsquaws rank among the world's most numerous ducks. Biologists believe the population is stable.

Hunting Strategies – The distinctive drake is prized by collectors. Oldsquaws are hunted with traditional sea duck techniques.

Eating Quality – Poor; the meat is dark and has a strong flavor.

Harlequin duck hen (left) and drake (right)

Harlequin Duck
(Histrionicus histrionicus)

Description – This sea duck rivals the wood duck as North America's most beautiful waterfowl. The drake has blue-gray plumage overall, with white streaks and patches, many bordered with black. The flanks are russet-colored, and the crown has a russet patch. The bill is bluish gray.

The hen is dark brown overall, with a white belly and white patches on the head. Both sexes have grayish legs, feet and bills. Juveniles resemble the adult hen.

Size – Drakes measure 16 to 21 inches long and weigh $1\frac{1}{3}$ to $1\frac{2}{3}$ pounds; hens, 14 to 17 inches and 1 to $1\frac{1}{3}$ pounds.

Migration – There are distinct Atlantic and Pacific populations of harlequins. Atlantic birds breed in

Iceland, Greenland and northeastern Canada; Pacific birds, from the central Rockies to northern Alaska. The fall migration, which occurs in September, involves a relatively short movement from breeding areas to coastal waters.

Habitat – Unique among diving ducks, harlequins prefer to nest around cold, fast-moving streams, often in mountainous regions. They winter along rocky seacoasts.

Food Habits – Crustaceans, mollusks, insects and fish comprise the bulk of the harlequin's diet. These birds dive and feed in turbulent waters, feeding along the bottom of swift streams and in heavy surf.

Breeding – These birds first breed as two-year-olds. The hen constructs a simple nest of grass, twigs and down, usually under a shrub or among rocks along a stream. She lays about 5 cream-colored eggs, which hatch in 28 to 30 days. While the hen nests, the drake defends against intruders.

Social Interaction – Harlequins usually are found in groups of no more than 12 birds. They spend much of their time loafing on rocks near water. The drake occasionally makes high-pitched squeaks, and the hen utters "ek-ek-ek-ek" calls.

Population – The Pacific population greatly outnumbers the Atlantic. Numbers of Atlantic birds have dropped so dramatically that the species is considered endangered. The cause of this decline is unknown.

Hunting Strategies – The birds are rarely hunted in the East, but in the West they are occasionally sought by specimen collectors, using traditional sea duck hunting techniques.

Eating Quality – Poor; the meat is dark and very strong-flavored.

Duck Wing Chart

Hunters often have a difficult time determining what kind of duck they've killed, even with the bird in hand. The difficulty in identifying ducks results from the multitude of similar species, the sex- and season-related variations within a given species and the fact that not all ducks are in the most identifiable plumage in hunting season.

While body colors vary widely, depending on molting stage, the wings undergo only minimal color changes. As a result, wing charts are the most reliable identification tool. The chart on the following pages is especially useful, because it features actual photographs, not drawings, of duck wings.

Learning to recognize duck silhouettes can also help in identification, especially in dim-light conditions.

Puddle ducks, as a rule, have more colorful wings than diving ducks. Puddle duck wings are shown on pages 64 to 67; diver wings on pages 68 to 71.

Primary coverts

Primaries

Puddle Ducks

Drake

Hen

Mallard – Easily identified by blue-violet speculum edged with white. Hen distinguished from drake by lighter edges around shoulder feathers, or *coverts*.

Lesser and
middle coverts,
or "shoulder"

Greater coverts

Secondaries

Speculum

Tertials

American Black Duck –
Like mallards, black
ducks have blue-violet
speculum, but it is edged
in black rather than white.
Tertials of hen darker than
those of drake, with lighter
edges.

Drake

Hen

Drake

Hen

Northern Pintail – Drake's speculum is iridescent green; hen's, brownish. Both speculums have white edge. Drake has gray shoulder; hen, brown with white-edged feathers.

Gadwall – Both sexes have white speculum, framed on top and one side by black. Drake's speculum much more noticeable than hen's, and shoulder shows splotch of cinnamon.

American Wigeon – Drake has prominent white shoulder and narrow, iridescent green speculum. Hen has smaller green speculum, and shoulder has brown feathers edged with white.

Wood Duck – Both sexes have blue speculum edged with white; hens have much wider white edge band than drakes, but band does not extend across tertials. Drakes have blue and black tertials; hens, brown.

**Blue-Winged Teal –
Cinnamon Teal –**
Drake of both species has
blue shoulder, white greater
coverts and iridescent
green speculum. Hen also
has blue shoulder, but
greater coverts are grayish
with white edges, and there
is no green speculum.

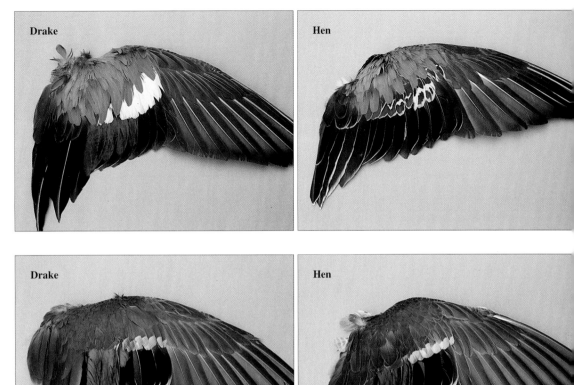

Drake | Hen

Green-Winged Teal –
Both sexes have iridescent
green speculum with adja-
cent black patch edged
with white. On drake,
black stripe on inner ter-
tial wider than that on
hen, and speculum is
slightly larger.

Northern Shoveler —
Drake has blue shoulder,
white greater coverts, and
iridescent, dark green
speculum. Hen has mottled
brown shoulder, white
greater coverts, and dull
green secondaries. Shoveler
is only duck with white-
shafted primary feathers.

Drake | Hen

Mottled Duck – Both
sexes have blue speculum
edged with black; specu-
lum of hen slightly less
intense.

Fulvous Whistling Duck –
Entire wing dark brown;
sexes nearly identical.

Mottled Duck

Fulvous Whistling
Duck

Diving Ducks

As a rule, diving ducks are more difficult to identify than puddle ducks, because there are so many species with similar black-and-white coloration. The lack of color explains why the majority of diving-duck wing charts are done in black and white. But there are subtle color variations that can help in identification, as the photographs on the following pages show.

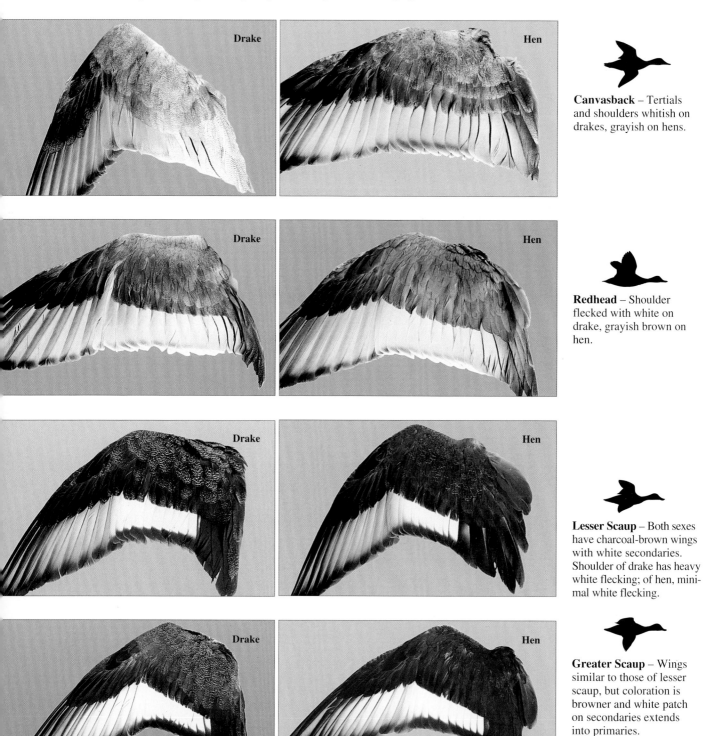

Canvasback – Tertials and shoulders whitish on drakes, grayish on hens.

Redhead – Shoulder flecked with white on drake, grayish brown on hen.

Lesser Scaup – Both sexes have charcoal-brown wings with white secondaries. Shoulder of drake has heavy white flecking; of hen, minimal white flecking.

Greater Scaup – Wings similar to those of lesser scaup, but coloration is browner and white patch on secondaries extends into primaries.

Ring-Necked Duck – Dark brownish wings have grayish secondaries. Sexes nearly identical, but wings of drake slightly darker.

Drake

Hen

Common Goldeneye – Drake has white secondaries and connecting white shoulder and greater coverts. Hen also has white secondaries, but shoulder separated from greater coverts by black.

Drake

Hen

Barrow's Goldeneye – Wings of both sexes resemble those of common goldeneye, but on drake, white shoulder and secondaries are separated. On hen, shoulders show slightly less white.

Drake

Hen

Drake

Hen

Bufflehead – Both sexes have white patch on secondaries, but drake has connecting white shoulder.

Drake

Ruddy Duck – Both sexes have identical all-brown wings.

69

Diving Ducks (continued)

Drake

Hen

Common Merganser – Drake has white shoulder patch, white secondaries and white inner tertials with narrow black edges. Hen has gray shoulder and tertials, and smaller white patch on secondaries.

Drake

Hen

Red-Breasted Merganser – On drake, white greater coverts separated from white secondaries and shoulder by black. Inner tertials white, with black edges. Hen's wings resemble those of common merganser.

Drake

Hen

Hooded Merganser – Drake has gray shoulder, and black-and-white-striped tertials and secondaries. Hen has brown shoulder, white-tipped greater coverts and black-and-white-striped secondaries and inner tertials.

Drake

Hen

White-Winged Scoter – Drake's wing all black, except for secondaries and tips of greater coverts. Hen's wing dark brown with similar white coloration.

Drake

Hen

Surf Scoter – Drake's wing all black; hen's, blackish brown.

Black Scoter – Wings resemble those of surf scoter, but hen's wing slightly lighter.

Common Eider – Drake has black wing with white shoulder and tertials. Hen has brown wing with mottled-brown shoulder, and white-tipped secondaries and greater coverts.

King Eider – Drake has black wing with white shoulder. Hen's wing similar to that of hen common eider, but darker brown with less pronounced white tips on feathers.

Oldsquaw – Drake's wing black, except for dark rusty brown secondaries. Hen's wing dark brown, with mottled-brown shoulder and slightly lighter secondaries.

Harlequin Duck – Both sexes have dark brown wings. Drake has iridescent blue speculum, dark blue shoulder and greater coverts with white spots, and white-and-brown-striped tertials.

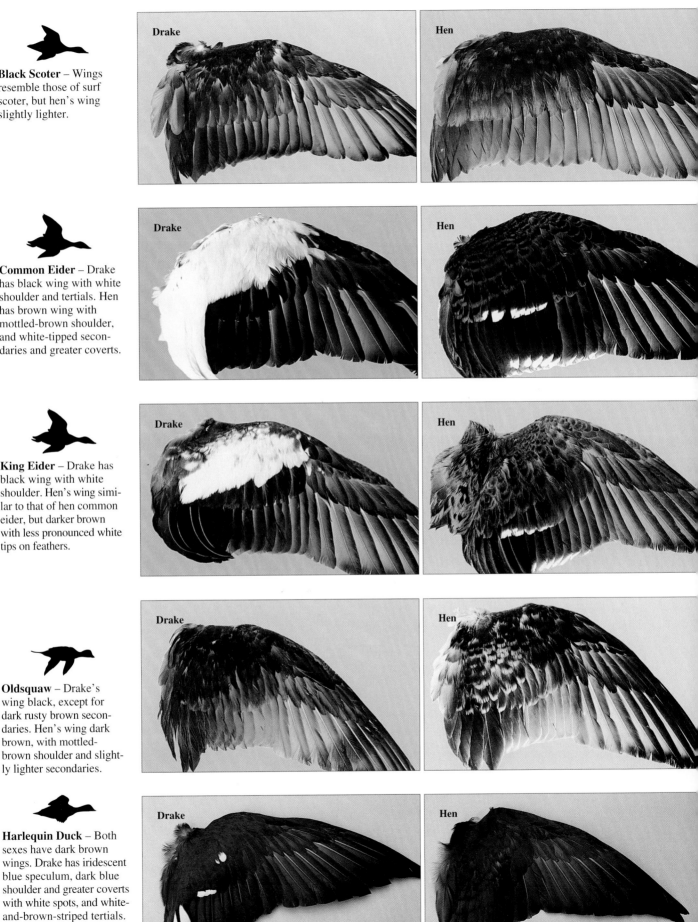

Drake

Hen

Drake

Hen

Drake

Hen

Drake

Hen

Drake

Hen

Upland Game Birds

Order Galliformes

Upland game birds spend most of their lives on high ground. This group includes grouse, quail, pheasants, partridges and ptarmigan. The wild turkey, though often considered big game, is classified as an upland game bird for the purposes of this book. All of these species, with the exception of the chukar and Hungarian partridges, are native to North America.

These birds have many adaptations that help them survive in upland habitat. Their four-toed feet give them good balance, and their stout beaks work well for picking seeds and other foods. Most of these birds, except for a few of the males, are colored in mottled earth tones – browns, grays and tans – which provide superb camouflage.

Upland game birds are primarily herbivores, feeding mainly on the leaves, stems and seeds of a variety of plants. They use their *crop*, which is an enlargement of their gullet, to store large quantities of seeds and other plant material for later digestion.

Except for the partridges and quail, upland game birds are *polygamous,* meaning that the male breeds with more than one female. Most males of polygamous species have elaborate breeding displays intended to attract mates. Nests are built on the ground, with the females relying on their drab camouflage to conceal themselves from predators.

Practically all upland game birds breed in their first year. Most are short-lived, seldom surviving beyond two years of age.

Most upland game birds do not migrate, although some species make minor movements from breeding to wintering grounds. A few species, such as doves and woodcock, are migratory, flying long distances between summer and winter ranges.

The popularity of upland game birds stems from their habit of exploding from cover and offering challenging wing shots. In most cases, you'll need a good bird dog to locate them and to find downed birds in heavy cover. To many hunters, the dog work is the most important part of the hunt.

Wild Turkey

(Meleagris gallopavo)

Common Name – Gobbler (male).

Description – Largest of the upland game bird species, the wild turkey is a dark bird with a naked, bluish head.

Eastern ■ Merriam's
Rio Grande ■ Florida
Gould's

The overall coloration of the male, or *tom*, is brownish black with an iridescent sheen. The wings have black and white barring. The long tail has a wide, black band near the end, with a tip of varying color. The tom has folds of red skin, called *wattles*, under the chin; fleshy, wartlike *caruncles* on the neck; and a fingerlike *snood* dangling beside the bill. A 4- to 10-inch projection of hairlike feathers, called a *beard*, extends from the breast.

The hen is smaller and browner than the tom, and lacks the tom's head adornments. The juvenile male, or *jake*, and the juvenile female, or *jenny*, resemble hens by fall, although they have a duller, more mottled color. But after the first year, jakes are larger than hens, and have begun to develop a beard.

Important Subspecies – There are five subspecies of wild turkey in North America:

• The eastern wild turkey (*M. gallopavo silvestris*) is the most abundant and most heavily hunted of the five subspecies. It is found throughout most of the eastern United States. Its population is increasing because of introductions, such as those in the Pacific Northwest and North Dakota. It has a copper-bronze sheen, and its tail has a chocolate-brown tip.

• Merriam's wild turkey (*M. gallopavo merriami*) is found in much of the western United States, from Montana to Arizona. It is the most adaptable of the five subspecies, and its numbers and range have grown due to stocking efforts. It has a purplish bronze sheen, and a buff-tipped tail.

• The Rio Grande wild turkey (*M. gallopavo intermedia*) is an open-country bird found primarily in the south-central United States from Nebraska through Texas and into Mexico. Its range has expanded westward thanks to stocking efforts. The overall

Eastern wild turkey tom; hen with young (inset)

body sheen is a pale copper, and the tail has a yellowish tip.

• The Florida wild turkey (*M. gallopavo osceola*) is found only in Florida, and has a relatively small, stable population. It is similar in appearance to the eastern wild turkey, but has darker wings and an iridescent, greenish gold body color. It may hybridize

with the eastern turkey, where the ranges of the two subspecies overlap.

• Gould's wild turkey (*M. gallopavo mexicana*) is found in extreme southern Arizona and New Mexico and into northern Mexico. It resembles the Merriam's subspecies, but has a bluish green sheen and a white-tipped tail. The population is stable.

Size – Toms measure 36 to 44 inches long and weigh 17 to 28 pounds; hens, 26 to 34 inches and 8 to 12 pounds. Subspecies vary slightly in size: the eastern wild turkey is the largest; the Florida, the smallest.

Habitat – Turkeys are birds of the big woods. An individual bird requires from a few hundred to more than a thousand acres of ground with a combination

Merriam's wild turkey

of trees for roosting, a reliable water source and an open feeding area. In spring and summer, when the birds are nesting and raising broods, they seek openings in or alongside the woods, with dense, grassy cover at least 3 feet high. In winter, they prefer more densely wooded habitat.

Birds in the East generally inhabit dense, mixed-hardwood forests and river bottomlands adjacent to agricultural lands. Birds in the West and South prefer pine and oak forests near streams. Florida birds are found in oak and pine woods, palmetto flats and cypress bottomlands.

Movement – Wild turkeys move seasonally between nesting and wintering areas, but seldom travel more than two miles.

In mountainous areas, wild turkeys occupy higher elevations in spring and summer, and lower elevations in fall and winter, sometimes moving as much as forty miles between ranges.

Food Habits – Opportunistic feeders, wild turkeys subsist mostly on plant material, including fruits, acorns and other nuts, small grains, and the seeds, shoots and roots of grasses and various other plants. They also eat many types of insects, small amphibians and even lizards. Turkeys generally fly down from roosting trees to feed in early morning, and return to the trees in the evening.

Breeding – Toms begin their breeding displays in early spring while still gathered in flocks in the wintering areas. With tail fanned, feathers fluffed and wing tips dragging, the tom struts boldly while emitting low-pitched hums. He repeats this display, coupled with the characteristic gobble call, until he attracts a hen. The most dominant toms breed with the majority of hens, continuing to display after each mated hen goes off to nest. By late spring, breeding is nearly

Florida wild turkey

complete and the male's display begins to taper off.

The hen becomes very secretive at nesting time, distancing herself from other hens. The nest site is usually under or near a log, bush or clump of vegetation. She scrapes a shallow depression, lines it with leaves and twigs, then lays 8 to 14 buff-colored, brown-speckled eggs, which hatch in about 27 days. The young *poults* grow quickly and can make short flights within 8 to 10 days.

Social Interaction – Wild turkeys gather in wintering flocks that range from less than a dozen to several hundred birds. In spring, just before the mating season, this large flock divides into three sexually segregated groups: one consisting of hens, another of jakes and a third of toms. In the latter, a single tom emerges to do most of the breeding.

Wild turkeys are extremely vocal birds with many different calls, particularly during the breeding season. Toms gobble and "putt," and hens yelp. Lost poults, and occasionally other birds, make "kee-kee" calls.

Population – Increasing. Because of restoration efforts by wildlife management agencies, North America has more wild turkeys now than it did during presettlement days. In some states where wild turkeys were once rare or absent, there are now huntable populations.

Hunting Strategies – Wild turkeys have excellent sight and hearing, making them one of the wariest of all game birds. A hunter dressed in full-body camouflage can successfully use calls to lure toms into gun range. Aim for the head and neck, because your shot may not penetrate the thick layer of body feathers.

Eating Quality – Excellent; many consider the meat better than that of domestic turkey.

Rio Grande wild turkey

Gould's wild turkey

Ringneck rooster

Ring-Necked Pheasant
(Phasianus colchicus)

Common Names – Ringneck, Chinese pheasant, English pheasant.

Description – The rooster, or cock, has a conspicuous white ring around the neck, an iridescent, greenish black head, and a red wattle around each eye. The breast is a dark reddish copper, the sides and back are a lighter copper, and the rump has a powdery blue patch. The tail is very long and pointed, and is barred along its entire length. The legs have a long, sharp spur.

The hen is mottled with brown and cream-colored feathers from head to tail. Toward the underside of the body, the mottling changes to a uniform beige.

The tail is noticeably shorter than the rooster's, and the legs do not have spurs.

Juveniles resemble adults by their first fall. On young males, the leg spurs are shorter, more rounded and lighter colored than on adult roosters.

Size – Roosters measure 30 to 36 inches long and weigh 2½ to 3 pounds; hens, 21 to 25 inches and 1¾ to 2¼ pounds.

Movement – These birds spend most of their lives in an area of a few hundred acres. When grasslands become snow-covered in winter, pheasants move to heavier cover in cattail sloughs, woodlots, brushy draws and river bottoms.

Habitat – Pheasants are found through many of the western and northern states, and portions of the Canadian prairie provinces. They are best suited to areas that have a good supply of small grains, and a mixture of grasslands, wetlands, and brushy or woody cover. The birds nest in most any grassy cover, including roadside ditches, railroad rights-of-way, hay fields, shelterbelts, and the edges of crop fields.

Ringneck hen

Food Habits – The diet consists mostly of small grains, such as corn, wheat, oats, milo, sorghum and soybeans, but pheasants also eat weed seeds and a variety of insects. The birds generally have a pre-dictable daily routine, which may vary depending on weather. In the morning, they move from roosting cover to feeding areas, where they spend an hour or two. For the midday hours, they move to light, grassy loafing cover. In the late afternoon, pheasants move back to feeding areas, returning to roosting cover at sunset. Winter storms may keep the birds in heavy cover throughout the day.

Breeding – In spring, roosters spread out into loose breeding territories. They crow at roughly 3-minute intervals to draw in hens. To entice a hen into breeding, a rooster struts around her with feathers ruffled and wattles swollen.

In a spot with grassy cover at least 6 inches high, the hen scrapes an oval depression into the ground and lines it with dry plant material and feathers. She lays 6 to 15 olive-brown eggs, which hatch in 23 to 25 days. A hen sometimes lays her eggs in the nest of another pheasant.

Social Interaction – Although generally solitary, pheasants may congregate in feeding fields. And in severe winter weather, they may form groups of up to several dozen birds. Roosters communicate with a loud, raspy "kaw kawk," and sometimes let out a series of cackles when flushed or alarmed. Hens are silent.

Population – Increasing. Numbers have increased since 1985, when the Conservation Reserve Program began converting millions of acres of farm land into idle grasslands, providing new nesting cover for pheasants.

Hunting Strategies – Early in the season, you can successfully hunt pheasants in short-grass loafing areas, but later in the hunting season the birds retreat into denser cover, such as cattail sloughs and brushy islands in swamps. Hunting is most productive when you use a dog to locate the birds and find them once they are down.

Eating Quality – Excellent; pheasants have tender, mild-tasting meat.

Hungarian Partridge

(Perdix perdix)

Common Names – Although the official name of this bird is the gray partridge, practically all hunters know it as the Hungarian partridge, or hun. It is also known as the hunkie and Bohemian partridge.

Description – This short, rotund bird is a blend of gray and brown colors. The head has a rust-colored mask, and the neck and throat are gray. The back is light brown with cream-colored streaks; the sides, gray with chestnut bars. The tail is a bright reddish brown, and the legs and feet are blue-gray. The sexes are similar in appearance, but most males have a chestnut-colored horseshoe on the breast. Juveniles resemble adults by early fall, though their legs and feet are yellow rather than blue-gray.

Size – Adults measure 12 to 14 inches long and weigh ¾ to 1 pound. Males are slightly larger than females.

Habitat – Hungarian partridges are found in open prairie regions of the northern United States and south-central Canada. Unlike most game birds, the hun uses grain fields and agricultural grasslands for nesting and roosting, as well as for feeding.

Movement – Hungarian partridges do not travel great distances. They usually stay within 50 feet of cover, and when flushed, they rarely fly more than 300 yards.

Food Habits – Cultivated grains – corn, wheat, oats and barley – comprise most of the Hungarian partridge's diet. Leafy greens and the seeds from weeds and grasses also are important foods.

Breeding – During the breeding display, the male struts in a circle, stretches his neck, and utters "keee-uk" chirps.

After breeding, the male stands guard while the female builds the nest, usually in a hay field or other grassy area. She digs a shallow scrape in the ground and lines it with dead vegetation and feathers. Clutches include 6 to 20 olive-colored eggs, which hatch in 23 to 25 days.

Social Interaction – Family coveys consist of the two parents and their offspring. In the fall, other birds may join the covey to form a group of more than 20 birds, which stays together until the spring breeding season. Hungarian partridges make a series of rapid chirps when flushed.

Population – Although the bird's annual numbers can be dramatically affected by weather, biologists believe the long-term population is stable.

Hunting Strategies – Because these birds are often found in wide-open cover, hunters are most successful if they use pointing dogs to locate them. Because huns fly only a short distance, you can follow the coveys and flush them several times.

Eating Quality – Excellent; the meat is somewhat dark but has a mild flavor.

Chukar Partridge

(Alectoris chukar)

Common Names – Rock partridge, red-legged partridge, redlegs.

Description – Similar in size and shape to the Hungarian partridge, the chukar is a grayish brown bird with dark diagonal bars on the flanks, and a distinctive black band that passes through the eye and runs down the throat. The throat and cheeks are white; the bill and legs, red.

The sexes are identical in appearance. Juveniles resemble adults by fall, though they are slightly smaller.

Size – Adults measure 12 to 15 inches long and weigh 1 to 1½ pounds.

Habitat – Chukar partridges are found mainly in the arid mountainous regions of the western United States and western Canada. They prefer rocky slopes covered with a mixture of grasses, weeds and sagebrush, and a nearby water source, such as a creek or spring seep.

Movement – Highly mobile birds, chukars may fly great distances, more than 30 miles, between summer and winter ranges. In winter, the birds descend to lower elevations to avoid heavy snows.

Food Habits – Leaves and seeds of grasses comprise most of the chukar partridge's diet. The bird is especially fond of cheatgrass, but also eats the leaves of sweet clover and alfalfa, and the seeds and fruits of many other plants.

Breeding – Although this species is not as territorial as most other upland game birds, the male uses his "chuk-chuk-chukara" call to deter other males as well as to attract mates. The male breeding ritual includes strutting, head-tilting and waltzing to draw females.

After breeding, the male selects a clump of vegetation for a nesting site and begins scraping out a depression. The hen completes the nest, then lays a clutch of 10 to 20 whitish, brown-speckled eggs, which hatch in about 25 days.

Social Interaction – After the broods hatch, two or more family groups join to form coveys of up to 40 birds. These coveys remain together until breeding time the following spring. Each covey has a *sentinel* that serves as a lookout.

The chukar's distinctive call is used not only at breeding time, but also to rally a broken-up covey.

Population – Slowly increasing; the bird's numbers are gradually rising, due to stocking efforts in several western states.

Hunting Strategies – Chukar partridges are renowned runners, often racing uphill instead of flushing when threatened. The best strategy is for a pair of hunters to walk along a slope, with one hunter positioned high and the other low. When birds running uphill encounter the upper hunter, they are forced to flush.

Eating Quality – Excellent; the taste is very similar to that of Hungarian partridge, but the breast meat is whiter.

Ruffed Grouse

(Bonasa umbellus)

Common Names – Ruff, wood grouse, drummer, partridge, pa'trige, willow partridge, pat.

Description – The ruffed grouse is easily distinguished from other woodland game birds by its long, rounded tail with a distinct black band near the end. The bird gets its name from the conspicuous patches of black feathers, or *ruffs,* on the neck.

The birds have two distinct color phases, both of which may occur in the same family. The red phase predominates in the southern part of the range; the gray phase, in the northern part and at high altitudes. Red-phase birds have a mottled, brownish body and chestnut-colored tail. Gray-phase birds have a mottled, grayish body and gray tail.

Males are identified by the unbroken black tail band. In females, this band is less distinct on the central two feathers (below). On both sexes, the legs are feathered down to the base of the toes. Juveniles resemble adults by fall, although they are slightly smaller.

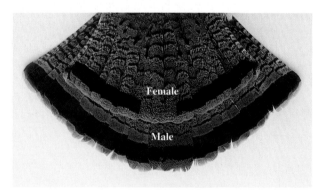

Comparison of male and female tails

Size – Adults measure 17 to 20 inches long and weigh 1 to 1½ pounds. Males are slightly larger than females.

Habitat – Found throughout most of Canada and Alaska, ruffed grouse also are present in much of the northern continental United States and throughout the Appalachians as far south as Georgia. Their favorite habitat is mixed-age woodlands with a combination of aspen, alder, birch, dogwood, hazel, beech and hornbeam, along with a few conifers. In the southern part of the range, the birds are found in woodlands with evergreen shrubs, such as holly, mountain laurel and rhododendron.

Grouse drumming on a log

Movement – These birds spend their lives in a very small area, usually no more than 40 acres. In early fall, however, young birds dispersing from their family groups may move up to 10 miles, an activity sometimes called the *fall shuffle.*

Food Habits – Ruffed grouse feed on the fruits, buds and catkins of a wide variety of trees and shrubs. Populations are highest in areas with plenty of aspens – preferably older male trees, since these offer the most nutritious buds.

Breeding – Males establish territories in early spring, when the snow begins to melt. To attract a mate, the male finds a perch atop an old log and begins *drumming,* making a series of wing beats that begins slowly and gradually accelerates. The noise resembles that of a one-cylinder engine starting up.

After breeding, the hen nests in a wooded area where there is a dense canopy to protect against hawks and owls and an open understory to let her spot approaching predators. She lays 8 to 14 buff-colored eggs in a shallow depression, usually against the base of a tree or in a clump of brush. The eggs hatch in about 24 days, and the chicks remain with the hen for 3 to 4 months before dispersing in the fall.

Social Interaction – Although ruffed grouse do not form coveys, small groups may congregate around a plentiful food source. In the winter, birds often group together to *snow roost* – diving into fluffy snow to keep warm and evade predators. Ruffed grouse are not particularly vocal, but females may squeal to warn chicks of danger, and both sexes may hiss to defend their territory.

Ruffed grouse in gray phase and red phase (inset).

Population – Cyclical. In much of their range, ruffed grouse undergo 10-year population cycles. Numbers in good years may be 15 times higher than in poor years.

Hunting Strategies – Because they tend to hold tight rather than flush when threatened, ruffed grouse are a favorite among pointing dog enthusiasts. A hunter without a dog can sometimes frighten a bird into flushing if he pauses for a few seconds near likely cover.

Eating Quality – Excellent; the breast meat is among the whitest of all game birds.

Sharp-Tailed Grouse
(Tympanuchus phasianellus)

Common Names –
Sharptail, sharpy, pintail grouse, prairie grouse, prairie chicken.

Description – Both sexes have an overall speckled appearance. The feathers are mottled with white, beige, brown and black; the undersides become increasingly whiter toward the abdomen and are lightly marked with brown Vs. The rump is white, with two brown central tail feathers that extend beyond the others. The legs and feet are feathered to the toes. A sharptail resembles a hen pheasant when flushed, but its shorter tail and white rump give it away in flight.

The male has a yellow comb and violet-colored gular sacs, which become more brilliant during the breeding season. The central tail feathers have lengthwise stripes. The female lacks the comb and gular sacs, and her central tail feathers are barred. Juveniles have whiter throats and shorter central tail feathers than adults, although they closely resemble adults by early fall.

Size – Adults measure 16 to 19 inches in length and weigh 1¾ to 2¼ pounds. Males are slightly larger than females.

Habitat – You can find sharptails throughout most of the Great Plains states, the prairie provinces of Canada, and much of Alaska. The best habitat consists of shortgrass prairie mixed with wood lots, shelterbelts, cultivated fields and abandoned farmsteads. They also inhabit semi-arid sagebrush country and forested areas, but are seldom found where more than 50 percent of the land is wooded.

Movement – Sharptails make seasonal movements of up to 25 miles from open grassy nesting areas to wintering areas with denser wooded cover. They are strong flyers and may travel a mile or more when flushed.

Food Habits – Preferred foods include small grains, clover, dandelion, the leaves and seeds of grasses, and insects. During fall and winter, sharptails also eat buds and berries. They sometimes travel several miles between feeding and roosting areas, although the distance is usually much less.

Breeding – The breeding ritual begins in early spring when the snow leaves the *leks* – the dancing grounds on which male sharptails perform their mating displays. Males compete for dominance by flutter-jumping and cackling, with the most dominant male occupying the center of the lek and attracting the most females. The male courts a female by strutting around her with tail fanned, head lowered and gular sacs inflated while making low-pitched cooing sounds.

Male sharptail displaying

After breeding, the hen nests in a field of alfalfa, clover, hay or grass, in a spot where the vegetation is at least 12 inches high, with brushy cover nearby. She scrapes a shallow depression in the ground, lines it

Male sharptail grouse

with grasses and feathers, then lays 8 to 15 buff-colored eggs, which hatch in 23 to 25 days.

Social Interaction – Sharptails live in family groups through the summer and fall. In late fall, families combine to form *packs* of a hundred or more birds, which remain together until the birds disperse to their breeding grounds in early spring.

The birds make a series of "tuk tuk tuk" calls when alarmed or flushed.

Population – Slightly declining. Although sharptails are doing well where there are good nesting areas, they have disappeared where farming and industry have reduced their habitat.

Hunting Strategies – The best time to hunt sharptails is early in the season, before they become wary and start grouping up. A dog, especially a wide-ranging pointer, can help locate birds in large grassy fields. After rousting a family group, you can track down individual birds and flush them.

Eating Quality – Good; the breast meat is dark but not particularly strong-tasting.

Prairie Chicken

(Tympanuchus spp.)

Common Names – Prairie grouse, prairie hen, chicken, pinnated grouse.

Description – Prairie chickens include two species of interest to hunters: the greater prairie chicken (*Tympanuchus cupido*) and the lesser prairie chicken (*Tympanuchus pallidicinctus*). Because the species are so similar, they are included together in this discussion.

■ Greater ■ Lesser

The prairie chicken is distinguished from other grouse by the male's long neck feathers, called *pinnae*, which become erect and resemble horns during the elaborate courting display. The bird's plumage is barred with beige and brown. The tail is short and rounded.

In males, the tail is barred across the center feathers only and has a black terminal band. In females, the tail is barred across the full width. The terminal band is not as dark, and the pinnae are barely noticeable. Juveniles resemble adults by fall.

Greater and lesser prairie chickens can be distinguished by their size and by the appearance of the gular sacs and pinnae. The greater prairie chicken, the more widespread species, has bright yellow gular sacs. The lesser is a smaller bird, with pale pink gular sacs and shorter pinnae.

Size – Adult greater prairie chickens measure 16 to 19 inches long and weigh 2¼ to 3 pounds; adult lessers, 15 to 17 inches and 1½ to 2 pounds.

Habitat – Greater prairie chickens are found in the tall-grass and mixed-grass prairies of the Midwest and the northern and central plains. Lesser prairie chickens inhabit the arid, shortgrass prairies in Kansas, New Mexico, and the Texas and Oklahoma panhandles.

Movement – Strong flyers, prairie chickens may travel up to 30 miles in search of wintering grounds with a reliable food source.

Food Habits – Small grains, such as wheat, soybeans, milo, sorghum and corn, are primary foods. The birds also eat alfalfa and the seeds and leaves of various prairie plants. Prairie chickens sometimes travel several miles between their grassland roosts and feeding grounds – flying out to feed before dawn, returning to their roosts for much of the day, then feeding again an hour or two before sunset.

Breeding – The prairie chicken is known for its spectacular courting display. The male dances and struts with his head low, wings held stiffly at his sides, pinnae flared and gular sacs inflated. He may also jump and flutter his wings. The male's booming call resonates through the gular sacs and can be heard a mile away, explaining why the courting areas are also called *booming grounds*. One dominant male breeds with most of the females.

Hens nest near the booming grounds. The greater prairie chicken hen lays 7 to 13 olive eggs with small brown spots in a depression in thick grass. The lesser hen lays 10 to 14 cream-colored eggs in a nest constructed at the base of a shrub. The eggs hatch in about 25 days.

Social Interaction – Birds stay in their family groups into fall, and gather in packs of up to 200 birds on the wintering grounds.

Population – Declining. Although six states have huntable populations, the prairie chicken's range has been vastly reduced as prairie grasslands were converted to agricultural use. However, the birds have been reintroduced into some areas of the northern Midwest.

Hunting Strategies – Early in the season, hunters comb grasslands with wide-ranging pointers. As the season progresses and the birds get more elusive, the best strategy is to pass-shoot from a blind set up between roosting and feeding areas. The birds often fly in to feed before sunrise, so start hunting early.

Eating Quality – Fair; the meat of the prairie chicken is very dark.

Greater prairie chicken male

Greater prairie chicken female

Lesser prairie chicken female

Lesser prairie chicken male

Sage Grouse

(Centrocercus urophasianus)

Sage grouse female

Common Names – Sage hen, sage turkey, sage cock, sage chicken.

Description – The sage grouse is a large bird, with a mottled grayish brown body and a black belly.

The male has long, narrow tail feathers, which form a distinctive fan during the breeding display. He has a white collar and black throat. The gular sacs are yellowish green.

The female has a more uniform color, a smaller black belly and no gular sacs. Both sexes have dark green legs and feet. By fall, juveniles resemble the adult females, although they are paler in color and have toes that are yellow rather than dark green.

Age and Growth – Males measure 26 to 30 inches long and weigh 5 to 7 pounds; females, 20 to 24 inches long and 3 to 4 pounds.

Habitat – Sage grouse are found primarily in the western mountain states, at altitudes of up to 9,000 feet. As its name suggests, the sage grouse relies on sagebrush for food and cover. It prefers slightly rolling country with large sagebrush flats and few trees or little tall brush to obstruct its vision. A reliable water source is essential, because rainfall amounts are generally low in this bird's range.

Movement – Sage grouse often move to lower elevations in winter, sometimes traveling as far as 20 miles.

Food Habits – Primary foods include the buds, leaves and shoots of sagebrush. In summer the birds also eat grasses, alfalfa, berries, small grains and insects. Sage grouse feed early and late in the day, bedding down in draws during midday.

When snow covers sagebrush at high altitudes, the birds seek food at lower elevations or on snow-free, windswept ridges.

Breeding – Like sharptail grouse and prairie chickens, the sage grouse puts on a spectacular communal courting display each spring. Large groups of birds gather on a single breeding ground, where the males fan their tails, strut and inflate their gular sacs to establish dominance over rivals. A few dominant males breed with most of the hens.

After breeding, the hen forms a nest by scratching a large depression beneath a sagebrush plant. She lays 6 to 9 olive-green eggs, which hatch in about 26 days.

Social Interaction – In early fall, groups of 2 to 4 hens and their broods often flock together. Hens without broods usually flock with males. By late fall, birds of both sexes and all ages congregate in packs of more than 100 birds, which remain together until the birds breed in spring.

Population – Cyclical. Sage grouse populations fluctuate in cycles of about 10 years. Their population seems to be related to that of jackrabbits. When jackrabbits are abundant, predators focus on them, allowing sage grouse numbers to climb.

Hunting Strategies – Sage grouse are usually hunted on sagebrush flats, usually near water holes or crop fields. Hunting is best early and late in the day, when the birds are feeding. These birds may flush wildly, so it pays to use close-working dogs.

Eating Quality – Young birds are mild-tasting, but old ones may have a strong, sagey flavor.

Sage grouse male

Blue Grouse
(Dendragapus obscurus)

Common Names – Mountain grouse, sooty grouse, dusky grouse, Richardson's grouse, pine grouse, hooter, fool hen.

Description – The blue grouse is noticeably larger than any of the other forest-dwelling grouse. The male has a bluish gray upper body, with brownish black under-sides and wings. The black tail usually is tipped with gray, and the rump is white. At breeding time, the male develops bright combs and gular sacs, varying in color from yellow to red.

The female has a brownish body and a brownish gray tail, with whitish mottling on the head, neck and wings. On both sexes, the legs are feathered down to the base of the toes. Juveniles resemble adult females by their first winter, though their tails usually are shorter.

Size – Males measure 19 to 23 inches long and weigh 2½ to 3 pounds; females, 17 to 20 inches long and 1½ to 2 pounds.

Habitat – Blue grouse are found mostly in the mountainous regions of the western United States and Canada, at elevations of 8,000 to 12,000 feet. They prefer areas with an abundance of conifers, which provide food and cover.

Movement – In late winter, blue grouse move to lower elevations to breed and raise their young. Males return to high country soon after breeding, but females and young birds remain at lower elevations until the young are old enough to fly.

Food Habits – These birds consume the needles, buds, seeds and twigs of conifers, particularly Douglas fir, throughout the year. In summer, they also eat leaves and berries of snowberry, elderberry and other bushes. Most feeding occurs early and late in the day.

Breeding – In spring, the male claims a territory by making owl-like hooting sounds, the call that earns him the common name *hooter*. On his breeding area, called the *hooting grounds,* the male attracts a mate by strutting about with tail fanned and gular sacs inflated. Once breeding is completed, he moves on to mate with other hens.

The hen nests among aspens, small shrubs or grasses. She scrapes out a depression in the ground, usually against a log or beneath low tree branches, where she lays 5 to 10 cream-colored, brown-speckled eggs, which hatch in about 26 days.

Social Interaction – Although blue grouse are solitary and do not form coveys, several birds may congregate to take shelter in an isolated clump of mature conifers.

Population – Stable; blue grouse numbers are much less cyclical than those of the ruffed grouse.

Hunting Strategies – Look for blue grouse in sparse stands of Douglas fir. Birds usually concentrate at a particular elevation, so once you locate them, continue to hunt at that level. Blue grouse generally sit tight when threatened, and in lightly hunted areas they may refuse to flush.

Eating Quality – Excellent; the white meat is similar in flavor to that of ruffed grouse.

Blue grouse male and female (inset)

Spruce Grouse
(Dendragapus canadensis)

Common Names – Fool hen, spruce partridge, Franklin grouse, Canada grouse, swamp grouse, black partridge.

Description – This bird is smaller than the blue grouse, and it lacks the crested head of the ruffed grouse.

The male has a brownish head and back, black throat and tail, and a red comb. The breast has white-tipped feathers with a distinct black splotch in the middle; the flanks are a lighter brown, with white streaks. In the eastern part of the range, the male has a chestnut tip on the tail.

The female has an overall brownish color, with lighter undersides mottled with dark brown. Juveniles resemble the adults by fall.

Size – Males measure 16 to 17 inches long and weigh 1 to 1¼ pounds; females, 15 to 16 inches and ¾ to 1 pound.

Habitat – In the United States, the bird's range includes the northern Rocky Mountain states, and portions of the Great Lakes states, New England, and the Pacific Northwest. The spruce grouse also is found across most of Canada and Alaska. The birds prefer forests with a mixture of pine, spruce, fir, aspen and birch, but they also may inhabit swampy and boggy areas.

Movement – Although spruce grouse generally stay within a range of 5 to 20 acres, a young male may travel more than a mile when establishing his own territory in the spring.

Food Habits – Adults feed mostly on the needles of conifers. They also eat a variety of berries and leaves, including those of the blueberry, huckleberry and snowberry.

Breeding – After establishing a breeding territory – usually in an area with a mixture of conifers, brush and open areas – the male attracts a female with a mating display that includes fanning his tail and strutting with wings drooped and red eye combs enlarged.

After breeding, the hen nests alone in a well-concealed area, usually in brush or under low tree branches. After scraping a small depression in the ground, she lays 5 to 9 buff-colored, brown-speckled eggs, which hatch in about 22 days.

Social Interaction – Family groups remain intact into the winter. Though not very vocal, the spruce grouse makes a series of low-pitched clucks when alarmed.

Population – Although little is known about actual numbers, the population is thought to be steady.

Hunting Strategies – Most spruce grouse are taken incidentally by hunters seeking ruffed or blue grouse. When threatened, the spruce grouse often hops into a tree rather than flushing – hence the common name, "fool hen."

Eating Quality – Fair; the meat is dark and may have a strong pine-needle flavor, especially in older birds.

Spruce grouse male and female (inset)

Willow Ptarmigan

(Lagopus lagopus)

Common Names – Alaska ptarmigan, snow grouse, Allen ptarmigan, Arctic grouse, willow grouse, red grouse (Scotland).

Description – A member of the grouse family, the willow ptarmigan is the largest of the ptarmigan species, and like other ptarmigan, it exhibits different seasonal plumages.

In summer, the bird has a chestnut-colored head and back, white wings and belly, and a red comb over each eye. The legs are feathered to the base of the toes. In winter, it is all white, except for a black tail, and the legs are feathered to the tips of the toes. The sexes are similar, but the hen lacks the combs above the eyes, and her summer plumage is grayer than the male's. Juveniles resemble adults by fall.

Size – Adults measure 15 to 17 inches long and weigh 1 1/4 to 1 1/2 pounds.

Habitat – The most widespread of all the ptarmigans, this bird is found throughout Alaska and most of the Canadian Arctic. As its name suggests, the willow ptarmigan spends much of its time in willow thickets found along rivers and streams. It also inhabits northern forests, mountain valleys and brushy foothills.

Movement – In winter, the birds move south into valleys, river bottoms and creek beds. When populations are dense, the birds may disperse southward as far as northern Minnesota.

Food Habits – Blueberries and crowberries are the most important summer foods. In fall and winter, the birds eat mostly buds and twigs of willow, as well as the buds and catkins of alder and birch.

Breeding – Males begin courtship and territorial displays in fall, and the behavior intensifies just before spring breeding. To defend his territory, a male approaches intruding males with body low, combs flared, head forward and mouth open. A male courts a female by fanning his tail, waltzing around her, stamping rapidly, bowing and wagging his head from

Willow ptarmigan in summer and winter (inset) plumage

side to side. As part of the courtship ritual, males perform a *song flight*, in which they make a loud "go-back, go-back, go-back" call.

The hen scrapes a shallow depression on a dry tundra location, and lines the nest with grasses and other plants. She lays 7 to 10 yellowish eggs with brown splotches, which hatch in about 22 days. These birds are monogamous, and the male helps defend the brood against intruders.

Social Interaction – During the winter, willow ptarmigan form sexually segregated flocks that may number in the thousands. Male flocks occupy open or alpine areas; female flocks are found in wooded locations. Like ruffed grouse, willow ptarmigan may snow roost by diving into snow for warmth and protection from predators.

In addition to the song flight call, these birds have more than a dozen other recognizable calls.

Population – Although numbers fluctuate dramatically from year to year, the population is stable over the long term.

Hunting Strategies – Look for these birds at the lower elevations of mountainous areas in late fall and early winter, when they are grouping up around willow thickets.

Eating Quality – Good; the dark meat is relatively mild-tasting, but can be tough in older birds.

Rock ptarmigan in winter and summer (inset) plumage

Rock Ptarmigan
(Lagopus mutus)

Common Names – Arctic grouse, barren-ground bird, snow grouse, white grouse, rocker.

Description – Like the willow ptarmigan, the rock ptarmigan has black outer tail feathers. In summer plumage, however, it is a mottled gray-brown rather than chestnut-colored. The belly and wings are mostly white. In winter plumage, the rock ptarmigan is all white, except for the dark outer tail feathers and a dark bar through the eye. The sexes are similar, but the male has red eye combs and may be slightly darker than the female in summer.

Size – Adults measure 12 to 14 inches long and weigh 1 to 1¼ pounds.

Habitat – Found throughout Alaska and most of northern Canada, the rock ptarmigan prefers upland tundra with heath or willow thickets. They are often found in hilly country well above the timberline.

Movement – Harsh winter conditions drive rock ptarmigan southward, but they seldom venture farther south than the tree line.

Food Habits – In summer, these birds eat the buds and flowers of dwarf birch, various berries, and the seeds and tips of horsetail. In winter, they feed on the buds and twigs of willow, and on dried leaves.

Breeding – Males defend territories as large as one square mile, engaging intruding males in vigorous aerial chases or violent ground battles. The male draws females by performing an elaborate song flight, in which he flies upward while making guttural clicking sounds, then settles back to the ground on spread wings. Finally, he runs forward, calling and bowing his head. A male may breed with two or more females.

The female builds a shallow nest within the male's territory, where she lays 6 to 9 buff-colored, brown-spotted eggs, which hatch in about 21 days. The male may help care for the chicks.

Social Interaction – As young birds mature, the families usually join with other broods and unattached adults to form packs that eventually number as many as 300 birds.

In winter, the birds dig roosting burrows in the snow, just deep enough to protect their bodies while leaving their heads exposed.

Population – Numbers fluctuate dramatically from year to year, but biologists believe the population is stable over the long term.

Hunting Strategies – Although seldom hunted because of the remote rocky terrain, the birds are sometimes taken by caribou hunters for camp meat.

Eating Quality – Good; identical to willow ptarmigan.

White-Tailed Ptarmigan
(Lagopus leucurus)

Common Names – Snow partridge, snow grouse.

Description – The white-tailed ptarmigan is distin-guished from the other ptarmigan by its completely white tail.

In summer, the head, neck, back and rump are mottled with buff, white and black; the undersides are white. In winter, the plumage turns all white. The sexes are similar, but the males have red eye combs and the mottling on the chest does not extend as far down the undersides.

Size – Adults measure 12 to 13 inches long and weigh ¾ to 1 pound.

Habitat – White-tailed ptarmigan are found in mountainous regions of the western United States, Alaska and Canada. In spring and summer, they inhabit alpine ridges and meadows up to 2,000 feet above the timberline, using low-growing willow, heath and mosses for cover. They winter at lower elevations where there is an abundance of willows.

Movement – In winter, birds move down to the vicinity of the timberline, which is generally no more than a few miles from their summer habitat.

Food Habits – Willow buds and twigs are the pri-mary foods. In spring and summer, the birds also eat a variety of green leaves and flowers, including cinquefoils, buttercups and saxifrage.

Breeding – Males defend their territories against other males through various intimidating displays and calls, both in the air and on the ground. In the *scream flight*, the airborne male utters a harsh four-syllable call. As a hen enters his territory, the male struts, bows his head and chases her.

White-tailed ptarmigan in summer and winter (inset) plumage

After breeding, the hen builds a shallow ground nest, lines it with grass and feathers, then lays 4 to 7 buff-colored eggs, which hatch in 22 to 23 days. The male may help the hen defend the nest, but she alone defends the chicks – often by hissing and attacking intruders with her wings extended.

Social Interaction – Early in the winter, white-tailed ptarmigan of both sexes may form flocks of up to 50 birds to feed on willow. Later, the sexes form segregated flocks, with females occupying lower elevations than males.

Population – Stable; white-tailed ptarmigan are rarely hunted and their remote habitat is not threat-ened by agriculture or development.

Hunting Strategies – In the open, treeless habitat of the white-tailed ptarmigan, you may be able to locate birds by using big-game techniques, such as glassing and stalking.

Eating Quality – Good; identical to willow ptarmigan.

Bobwhite Quail
(Colinus virginianus)

Common Names – Bobs, partridge, quail, American colin.

Description – This small, chunky game bird has a mottled brown back and wings, and a grayish tail. On the cock, the face is patterned with white and black; on the hen, white and buff.

Size – Adults measure 9 to 10 inches long and weigh 6 to 8 ounces.

Habitat – Bobwhite quail live in brushlands, abandoned fields and open pine lands throughout most of the eastern half of the United States and into Mexico. They also have been introduced into Idaho, Oregon and Washington. Bobwhites are better adapted to cold weather than other quail, but can thrive in hot, semi-arid climates, if they have a reliable water source.

Movement – The birds generally spend their entire lives in an area of 40 acres or less.

Food Habits – This bird feeds on hundreds of different kinds of plant seeds, mainly those of grasses, forbs and legumes. They also eat acorns, pine seeds, berries, soybeans, corn and insects.

Bobwhite quail hen

Bobwhites typically feed in crop fields and meadows both early and late in the day, taking cover in wood lots, bottom lands and ditches during midday. In dry areas, the birds generally feed near streams, ponds and man-made watering devices.

Breeding – After attracting a hen with his namesake call, a whistled "bob-bob-white," the male scratches out a shallow nest in grassy or brushy ground. He lines the nest with grass and covers part of it with a grassy dome. The hen then lays 12 to 16 eggs, which hatch in about 23 days.

Social Interaction – Bobwhites normally gather in coveys of 10 to 15 birds. When roosting, they sit on the ground in a ring, facing outward with tails together, allowing them to conserve energy and watch for predators.

Besides the familiar "bob-bob-white" call, the birds make a "whoo-ee-whoo" rallying call to regroup a broken-up covey.

Population – Declining. This bird's numbers have dropped in recent decades, due to the loss of small farms and the trend toward "clean farming," which has reduced thickets and weedy cover.

Hunting Strategies – A typical quail hunt involves using a wide-ranging pointing dog to pin down coveys so hunters can approach for close shots. When a covey is flushed, carefully mark the location of individual birds. They will usually hold tight for a second flush.

Eating Quality – Excellent; the white breast meat is among the tastiest of all upland birds.

Bobwhite quail cock

California quail male (left) and female (right)

California Quail
(Callipepla californica)

Common Names – Valley quail, topknot quail, blue quail.

Description – This species is distinguished from all other quail by the combination of a teardrop-shaped plume and scaled markings on the lower breast and abdomen. The sexes are similar in body color, with blue-gray chests and backs, and brownish flanks. But the male has a

much longer plume than the female, and his throat is black, outlined with white. Juveniles resemble females, although their plumes are shorter and lighter and their forehead feathers have pale gray terminal spots.

Size – Adults measure 9 to 11 inches long and weigh 6 to 7 ounces. Males are slightly larger than females.

Habitat – This species adapts to a wide range of conditions and can be found in most of the far western states and the Baja Peninsula. California quail inhabit valleys and foothills at elevations up to 4,000 feet. They are most prevalent in grasslands, savannahs and woodland openings where there is access to standing water.

Movement – The birds hold close to cover, rarely venturing far into the open, even when feeding. In winter, they move into areas with denser cover. California quail generally remain in an area 5 to 20

acres in size, although they sometimes travel more than a mile between their summer and winter ranges.

Food Habits – Seeds, fruits and leaves of forbs and grasses are the primary foods. The birds also feed on wheat and other small grains, and on the seeds and leaves of clover and alfalfa.

Breeding – After breeding, the mating pair leaves the wintering flock to find a nest site. The birds usually nest on the ground, in a shallow grass-lined depression, but they also have been known to nest in low shrubs. The female lays 9 to 15 cream-colored, brown-speckled eggs, which hatch in about 23 days. The hen tends the nest, though the male will take over if the hen is killed. Both parents care for the brood after the eggs hatch.

Social Interaction – Coveys number up to 50 birds during the hunting season. These coveys may combine to form wintering flocks of up to 500 birds.

The birds make a variety of calls, including the three-note rallying call: "chi-ca-go."

Population – Numbers fluctuate widely, increasing in years with adequate rainfall and decreasing in dry years, but the population is stable over the long term. Attempts to introduce the California quail in other regions have met with limited success, extending the bird's range slightly eastward.

Hunting Strategies – You will find most birds along field edges, in blackberry thickets, and in brushy cover along creek bottoms and around water holes. In open cover where quail tend to run instead of flush, the best strategy is to rush the covey to break it up, and then use a pointing dog to pin down singles and doubles.

Eating Quality – Excellent; similar in taste to bobwhite quail.

Gambel's Quail
(Callipepla gambelii)

Gambel's quail female

Common Names – Desert quail, Arizona quail.

Description – With its teardrop-shaped plume, the Gambel's quail resembles the closely related California quail, but does not have its scale-like belly feathers. The male has a dark facial mask outlined in white, and a black belly patch; the female lacks both features. By fall, juveniles look much like adults.

Size – Adults measure 9 to 11 inches long and weigh 5½ to 6½ ounces. Males are slightly larger than females.

Habitat – Among the desert quail – a group that also includes the scaled and Mearn's quail – the Gambel's is the most tolerant of hot, dry conditions, and the most vulnerable to cold. It is found in the extreme southwestern United States and western Mexico.

The most stable populations are found along the bases of desert mountains, where consistent rainfall produces the early, nutritious plant growth that hens need to lay large clutches. The best habitat has a mix of mesquite, Apache plume, catclaw, hackberry, creosote bush and saltbush, which the birds use for food and cover. They prefer taller, thicker cover than that used by scaled quail.

Movement – These birds rarely travel long distances, even in dry years, because they can get adequate water from succulent plants.

Gambel's quail male

Food Habits – Mesquite beans, juniper berries, prickly pear fruit and the seeds of various forbs and grasses are primary foods. The birds also will feed on the leaves, flowers and seeds of legumes, including alfalfa and clover.

Breeding – In spring, these monogamous birds form breeding pairs and leave winter flocks for nesting sites. In a shallow depression in the shade of a shrub or other vegetation, the hen lays 9 to 15 buff-colored, brown-spotted eggs, which hatch in about 22 days. While the hen incubates the eggs, the male remains nearby to defend the nest.

Social Interaction – Gambel's quail tend to form loose coveys, and when threatened they may flush individually rather than as a group. Birds in a broken-up covey utter a four-note "chi-ca-go-go" rallying call to regroup. During the hunting season, a typical covey consists of 10 to 40 birds, but by late fall groups may number more than 100.

Population – Annual numbers are directly related to winter and spring rainfall amounts, but over the long term, the population has remained steady.

Hunting Strategies – The species is renowned for running, especially on the hard, sparsely vegetated desert floor. For this reason, most hunters confine their efforts to heavy grass and brush, where the birds tend to sit tighter. Dogs are valuable if you are working heavy cover; short-haired pointers are best, because they can tolerate hot conditions.

Eating Quality – Excellent; the breast meat is white and tender.

Scaled Quail
(Callipepla squamata)

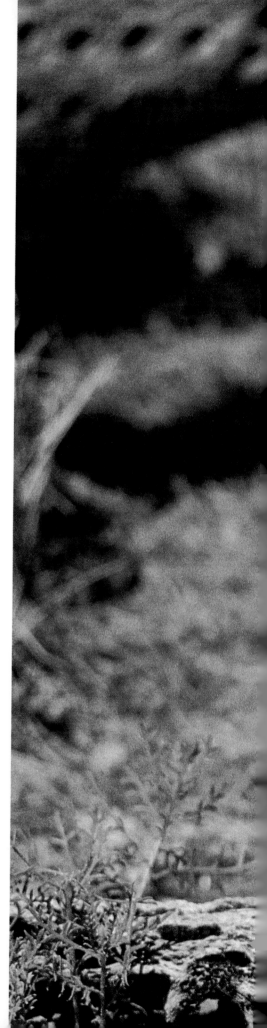

Common Names – Scalie, blue quail, blue, blue racer, cottontop.

Description – The scaled quail is a bluish gray color, with dark-edged breast feathers that give the appearance of scales. The crest is topped with buff or white.

Sexes are similar in plumage, though the male's crest is slightly longer and whiter than the female's. Juveniles reach adult appearance by fall.

Size – Adults measure 10 to 12 inches long and weigh 6 to 7 ounces. Males are slightly larger than females.

Habitat – Arid southwestern grasslands at elevations of 3,000 to 5,000 feet are the primary habitat of these desert quail. They are found from southern Kansas into central Mexico, and have been introduced into Washington and Nevada. The birds depend on grasses for food and cover, and also seek cover in cactus, mesquite and yucca. They must have access to a water source, such as a creek or water hole.

Movement – Scaled quail spend most of their lives in an area less than 80 acres, but in dry conditions, they move as far as necessary to find water.

Food Habits – Scaled quail feed on the seeds of native grasses and forbs; they also eat small grains, including sorghum, wheat and corn.

Breeding – The hen scratches out a shallow nest beneath a bush and lines it with grass. She lays from 8 to 12 eggs, which hatch in about 22 days.

Social Interaction – During the fall, birds gather into coveys numbering 10 to 30 birds; by winter these flocks may include more than 100. When a covey breaks up, the birds sound a "pey-cos" rallying call.

Population – Scaled quail numbers vary widely from year to year, increasing when there is ample summer rain. In extremely dry years, when water and food are scarce, the birds may not even attempt to nest. Over the long term, the scaled quail population is stable.

Hunting Strategies – Like Gambel's quail, these birds tend to run instead of flush. The best strategy is to rush them to break up the covey, then pursue singles, which will hold much tighter. You can also use pointing dogs if the cover is thick enough for the birds to hold in.

Eating Quality – Excellent; the white meat is similar in taste to that of bobwhite quail.

Mearn's Quail
(Cyrtonyx montezumae)

Common Names – Painted quail, fool's quail, harlequin quail, Montezuma quail, Massena quail.

Description – The male Mearn's quail has a complex black and white facial mask with no plume. The crest is rusty colored, the chest and undersides are black, and the flanks are heavily spotted with white or cinnamon.

The female is a buff or cinnamon color, and her facial pattern is much more subtle than the male's, with a whitish chin and throat. Both sexes have light-colored streaks on the wings. Juveniles usually resemble the adults by fall.

Size – Adults measure 8 to 9 inches long and weigh 5 to 7 ounces. Males are slightly larger than females.

Habitat – The range of this desert quail extends from southern Arizona, New Mexico and Texas southward far into Mexico. Mearn's quail inhabit dry, mountainous terrain at altitudes of 3,500 to 9,000 feet. They favor grassy valleys and ridges with scattered junipers and live oak, avoiding areas that are overgrazed.

Movement – Mearn's quail spend most of their lives in an area of no more than 10 acres.

Food Habits – These birds eat mostly tubers and bulbs, which they scratch from the ground using their strong legs and long claws. They also feed on acorns, seeds, berries and insects.

Coveys have predictable daily movements, roosting near the bottoms of ridges and working their way up hillsides as the day progresses, scratching for food along the way.

Breeding – Like other quail, the Mearn's is monogamous. Nesting later than most other upland birds, the female scrapes a shallow depression in dense, grassy cover, and lines it with vegetation to form a partial dome. The male stays nearby and sometimes assists with nest construction. The hen lays 8 to 14 white eggs, which hatch in about 26 days.

Social Interaction – Mearn's quail generally stay in family coveys of 6 to 12 birds, which remain together through the winter. Birds from a broken-up covey locate each other by making soft whinnying calls. The birds may form roosting rings to keep warm and watch for predators.

Population – Mearn's quail populations fluctuate from year to year, becoming more numerous when favorable summer rains increase food supplies. Although their range has shrunk over the years, the population is now relatively stable.

Hunting Strategies – Unlike most other desert quail, Mearn's quail hold extremely tight, making them popular among pointing dog enthusiasts. Once you flush a covey, you'll know where to find it next time, because the bird's home range is very small.

Eating Quality – Excellent; similar to bobwhite.

Mearn's quail male and female (inset)

Mountain Quail
(Oreortyx pictus)

Common Names –
Mountain partridge, plumed quail.

Description – This bird, the largest of the North American quail, is characterized by its long, straight head plume. The chest, neck and head are blue-gray; the back, olive; the belly and throat, chestnut with white bars. The

sexes are similar in appearance, though the females are duller in color. Juveniles resemble adults by fall.

Size – Adults measure 10 to 12 inches long and weigh 8 to 10 ounces. Males are slightly larger than females.

Habitat – These birds are found in mountainous regions of the far western states at altitudes up to 10,000 feet. At high elevations they can be found in brushlands mixed with tall conifers; at low elevations, in brushlands with scrub oaks, thorny bushes and shrubs.

Movement – Mountain quail move as much as 20 miles from breeding areas at high elevation to wintering areas in protected valleys.

Food Habits – These birds subsist mostly on fruits and berries, including wild grape, serviceberry, snowberry, hackberry and manzanita berry. Other foods include acorns, grasses, tubers, bulbs, seeds of various forbs, and some insects.

Breeding – The birds are monogamous, with the male whistling from a stump or other high perch to attract a female. After breeding, the hen builds a nest beneath a log or next to a rock or clump of weeds, and lays 8 to 12 reddish eggs, which hatch in about 25 days. The male protects the nest during incubation.

Social Interaction – Mountain quail spend most of their time in family coveys numbering fewer than 10 birds. In late summer, nonbreeding adults join the covey; in fall, several coveys join together to form a wintering flock of up to 60 birds. Mountain quail sound a softly whistled "wh-wh-wh-wh-wh-wh" as a rallying call to regroup a broken-up covey.

Population – Stable; this bird's numbers do not fluctuate as widely as those of other quail species.

Hunting Strategies – Because of the rugged terrain they inhabit, mountain quail are lightly hunted. Look for the birds around water holes or spring seeps, where they may be concentrated. Another easy way to locate birds is to listen for their rallying call.

A close-working pointer can pin down a covey in heavy cover while you position yourself for a shot.

Eating Quality – Excellent; the tender, white breast meat resembles that of bobwhite.

Migratory Upland Game Birds

This group, which includes woodcock, snipe, doves and pigeons, differs from other upland birds in that they migrate considerable distances between winter and summer ranges.

Woodcock
(Scolopax minor)

Common Names – Timberdoodle, woody, wood snipe, bec, bog snipe, bog sucker.

Description – The woodcock is a small, rotund bird with a long bill and large eyes positioned far back on the head. Well camouflaged, the woodcock is mottled with brown, black and rust colors, and has black barring across the top of the head. The sexes bear a close resemblance, although the female is slightly larger and has a longer bill. Juveniles resemble adults by early fall.

Size – Males measure 10 to 11 inches long and weigh 4½ to 7 ounces; females, 11 to 12 inches and 6 to 9 ounces.

Migration – Woodcock breed in much of the eastern half of the United States, and most of southeastern Canada. Fall migration in the northern part of the range begins in early October and continues through early December, as freezing ground pushes the birds southward. Woodcock migrate at night, usually riding on the strong, northerly winds associated with cold fronts. They begin arriving on the wintering areas in mid-November.

Habitat – The birds favor moist woodlands and bottomlands with a mixture of thickets and clearings. During the nesting season, they prefer forests of young aspen mixed with alder, and are often found near streams and swampy areas. In winter, the birds inhabit river bottomlands with hardwoods and a brushy understory.

Woodcock winter in most of the southeastern United States and along the Atlantic coast as far north as Rhode Island.

Food Habits – This bird feeds almost exclusively on earthworms, grubs and other invertebrates, using its long bill to probe in soft soil. The bill has a flexible tip, and the tongue and upper mandible are rough, letting the bird grasp its food underground. Because its eyes are set so far back on the head, the woodcock can easily spot predators while feeding.

Breeding – The male is known for its spectacular courtship flight. After arriving on the breeding grounds, he establishes and defends a territory, or *singing ground*, usually along the edge of a field or woodland opening. The courtship flight, performed at dawn and dusk, begins on the ground with the male

making "bzzt, bzzt, bzzt" sounds while strutting about and bobbing his head. Next, he flies vertically in decreasing spirals, levels off and circles high above the ground, finally descending to the ground while uttering "chickaree, chickaree" calls. The male usually mates with more than one female.

After breeding, the female goes off to nest and raise the young on her own. She scrapes a shallow depression in the ground, usually at the base of a small bush or tree located in or around a thicket, then lays 3 to 4 buff-colored eggs, which hatch in about 21 days. When threatened, the hen relies on her superb camouflage, sitting tight on the nest until the danger passes.

Social Interaction – Woodcock are solitary birds, although they may gather in small groups during the spring and fall migration.

Population – Declining; logging on the bird's breeding grounds is responsible for the diminishing numbers.

Hunting Strategies – The best time to hunt these birds is during the peak migration. Woodcocks leave conspicuous sign in the form of chalk marks, or *whitewash*, on the ground. It washes away easily, so finding whitewash tells you that woodcocks have been in the area very recently.

Because woodcock generally hide by remaining motionless and holding tight, they are ideal for hunting with a pointing dog.

Eating Quality – Fair; the breast meat is very dark, with a liverlike taste.

Common Snipe

(Gallinago gallinago)

Common Names – Wilson's snipe, jacksnipe.

Description – The snipe is a mottled, brown and white bird, with a very long bill that gets darker near the tip. The head and cheeks are striped with white and dark brown; the tail is rust-colored and fringed with white. The undersides are white, becoming streaked with brown toward the chest. The sexes are nearly identical, although females tend to be slightly larger and may have a longer bill. By fall, juveniles closely resemble adult birds.

Size – Adults measure 10 to 11 inches long and weigh 3½ to 5 ounces.

Migration – The breeding range includes the northern half of the United States, the far western states and most of Alaska and Canada. Juveniles begin the fall migration in late August, with adult birds leaving a week or two later. Snipe begin arriving on their wintering grounds in mid-October. Snipe winter in the southern United States, the far western states, Mexico, and along the Pacific coast of Canada to the Alaskan Peninsula.

Habitat – These birds nest in grasses and sedges adjacent to wetlands. They favor bogs and other wetlands with low, sparse vegetation. Snipe also inhabit flooded fields and wet pastures, and even roadside ditches.

Food Habits – The snipe uses its long, flexible bill to probe moist soil and shallow pools for insects, earthworms, mollusks and other invertebrates. They also feed on plant seeds.

Breeding – Males reach the breeding grounds and establish territories a week or two before the hens arrive. During the courtship display, the male makes vertical flights of up to 200 feet while whinnying and bleating, then flutters back to the ground. The flight is repeated until he attracts a mate.

After breeding, the female chooses a nesting site at the edge of a bog or sedge meadow, usually near alders or other low-growing shrubs. She scrapes a shallow depression, lines it with layers of dead grass, then lays 3 to 4 buff-colored, heavily blotched eggs, which hatch in about 19 days. Both parents help raise the chicks.

Social Interaction – Adults form small groups of 4 to 12 birds in the fall and winter. Snipe seldom gather in large flocks, except when migrating.

Although not very vocal, snipe emit a raspy "scaip" sound when alarmed or flushed.

Population – Stable; the snipe's ability to use many types of habitat keeps its numbers steady.

Hunting Strategies – Most snipe are taken incidentally by hunters seeking woodcock or grouse. Hunters looking for snipe usually walk the edges of flooded fields and low, grassy marshes during the peak of the fall migration.

The annual harvest of snipe is a fraction of what it was in the early 1900s, when an individual hunter commonly shot hundreds of snipe in a day and thousands in a season.

Eating Quality – Fair; the meat is very similar to that of the woodcock.

Mourning Dove
(Zenaida macroura)

Common Names – Turtle dove, dove.

Description – The mourning dove is the most common of the North American doves. It has a slim body and long, tapered tail that distinguish it from other doves. The male and female are nearly identical, with a fawn-colored neck and undersides. The

back and tail are slate gray to grayish brown, and the wings have black spots. The feet are red. Juveniles resemble adults by fall, but are slightly smaller.

Age and Growth – Adults measure 11 to 13 inches long and weigh 3½ to 5 ounces.

Migration – The breeding range runs from southern Canada and into Mexico. Because mourning doves are unable to tolerate cold weather, the fall migration in the northern part of the range begins as early as late August. Most birds reach their wintering grounds in Mexico and the southern United States in October and November. Southern birds do not migrate.

Habitat – Mourning doves can adapt to almost any upland habitat, with the exception of dense woods. They are common in urban and agricultural areas.

Food Habits – These doves feed heavily on seeds, including those of doveweed, foxtail, ragweed and wild hemp. At harvest time, they visit crop fields to feed on small grains.

Mourning doves typically fly from roosting trees to open feeding fields in morning, return to the trees at midday, and fly back to feeding areas in late afternoon. After feeding, they pick up grit, then fly to watering holes before roosting.

Breeding – After establishing a territory, the male attracts a mate by cooing and making display flights, consisting of noisy wing beats followed by glides.

The hen builds a nest of loosely arranged sticks, usually in a tree or shrub, but sometimes on the ground or even on a building ledge. She lays 2 to 3 white eggs, which hatch in about 15 days. Both parents care for the young, feeding them *crop milk*, a high-protein, milklike substance secreted from the crop. Mourning doves may raise several broods in one season.

Social Interaction – In the fall, the birds gather in migrating flocks numbering as many as 100 birds.

The mournful mating call, for which the bird is named, is a 5- to 7-note cooing sound.

Population – Stable. Because the birds often raise multiple broods and adapt so well to different habitats, populations easily withstand bad weather, predators and other threats. Mourning doves are the most numerous of all North American game birds.

Hunting Strategies – The usual technique is to pass-shoot these fast, acrobatic birds as they fly into feeding or watering areas. Many hunters use dove decoys to draw the birds into shooting range. Despite their tremendous popularity throughout most of the country, doves cannot be taken in several northern states.

Eating Quality – Good; the breast is dark but fairly mild-tasting.

White-Winged Dove
(Zenaida asiatica)

The white-winged dove is grayish brown, with white-edged wings and a distinctive blue eye ring. The squarish tail has white corners that are visible in flight. The sexes are similar, although males are slightly larger and more brightly colored. Whitewings weigh 5 to 6 ounces, and are about 12 inches long.

The bird's range extends from the southwestern United States, through Mexico and central America, and into South America. White-winged doves have been introduced into southern Florida. In fall, birds breeding in North America form large migration flocks, which fly to wintering areas along the Pacific coast of Mexico and Central America. The Florida population does not migrate.

White-winged doves favor open woodlands, citrus groves, brushlands and wooded urban areas. They feed on fruit, but they also eat various seeds and grains, including sunflower, corn, safflower and wheat.

The hen typically builds a nest of loose twigs in a low bush, where she lays about two buff-colored eggs. Both parents feed the young by regurgitating crop milk.

Whitewings are hunted most heavily in northeastern Mexico, usually by pass-shooting them along the edges of crop fields. They taste much like mourning dove.

White-Tipped Dove
(Leptotila verreauxi)

This dove has a light gray body, with darker gray wings and tail. The tail has white outer feathers, and the undersides of the wings are rust-colored. It is about the same size as the white-winged dove.

The whitetip is found in southern Texas, Mexico and Central America. Unlike other North American doves, it does not migrate.

The birds frequently occupy cleared areas that have grown back to dense brush. They prefer to remain near the wooded margins, rarely venturing into the open.

White-tipped doves eat seeds and fruits of forbs and trees, and also may feed in fields of sorghum, corn and sunflowers.

Although the female usually lays only two eggs, the nesting success rate is high, possibly because she builds a more substantial nest than do other species of doves.

Most white-tipped doves are taken incidentally by hunters seeking other doves. The taste resembles that of the mourning dove.

Band-Tailed Pigeon
(Columba fasciata)

The band-tailed pigeon is bluish gray with a dark band across the tail and a white band across the back of the neck. It weighs 9 to 12 ounces and is about 14 inches long.

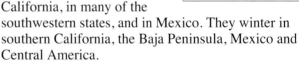

Bandtails breed near the Pacific coast from British Columbia to southern California, in many of the southwestern states, and in Mexico. They winter in southern California, the Baja Peninsula, Mexico and Central America.

These birds prefer coniferous forests, especially those with oak trees for roosting and feeding. They eat acorns and the buds and flowers of various shrubs and trees, as well as crops, including olives, cherries, grapes, corn, oats, peas and wheat.

The female's nest consists of a loose assembly of twigs, usually in a conifer tree. She generally lays a single egg.

Hunters usually pass-shoot these birds along the fringes of oak forests. The meat is much like that of mourning dove.

Marsh & Shoreline Birds

Order Gruiformes

This group of birds includes the cranes, coots and gallinules, and rails. These birds generally are waders, with long legs and widespread toes that allow them to walk easily along muddy bottoms and on matted aquatic vegetation. They spend much of their lives between the dry land of the upland game birds and the open waters of the waterfowl – in the muddy shoreline areas and fringes of shallow marshes.

These birds are *omnivores*, feeding on both plant and animal life. Most have bills that are longer and more pointed than those of waterfowl – ideal for feeding in densely weeded, shallow waters. All of these birds

migrate, and are considered migratory game birds for regulatory purposes.

Cranes are the tallest of all game birds. Of the two cranes found in North America, only the sandhill crane is hunted. The other species, the whooping crane, was once near extinction and is still on the endangered species list. Cranes are often confused with herons, but they lack the heron's crested head, and fly with necks extended rather than tucked in.

Coots and gallinules (including the moorhen) are characterized by a *frontal shield*, a bony extension of the bill that runs up the forehead. Unlike the other marsh and shoreline birds, they are good swimmers.

The rails are the smallest of this group. They have narrow, compact bodies that are ideal for wading through dense, emergent vegetation. Secretive birds, they are more apt to hide in dense vegetation than to fly when threatened. Because of their short, rounded wings, rails are poor flyers, and when flushed, they seldom fly long distances.

Sandhill Crane

(Grus canadensis)

Common Names – Crane, brown crane.

Description – The sandhill crane has both an extremely long neck and very long legs – a unique combination among game birds. The male and female are identical in appearance, with a dull gray overall body color, a red crown, and a long, dark gray bill. The rump  is covered by a tuft of bushy feathers. Juveniles are a rusty color, and lack the adult's red crown.

Size – Adults measure 35 to 45 inches long and weigh up to 12 pounds. Males are slightly larger than females.

Migration – The primary breeding range runs from Alaska, through northern and central Canada, and into the Great Lakes states. Smaller breeding concentrations are found in Mississippi, Georgia, Florida and some of the Rocky Mountain states. Birds in the northern part of the range begin to migrate in late August, after the young birds mature.

Sandhill cranes arrive on the wintering grounds from late October through December. Most winter along the Gulf Coast of Florida and Texas and in Mexico, but smaller concentrations are found in the southwestern states. Birds breeding in Florida do not migrate.

Habitat – Sandhill cranes inhabit shallow, open wetlands during the nesting season, and they winter on prairies, sedge meadows and farm pastures. During the migration, they often are found on partially dried-out lake beds, and along shallow rivers – especially those with sandbars and islands for roosting.

Food Habits – This bird feeds mostly on the shoots and seeds of a wide variety of marsh and meadow plants. In late summer, grasshoppers and other insects are important food sources, and during the fall migration the birds rely heavily on small grains. In winter, they feed on freshly sprouted corn and wheat.

During migration and while on the wintering grounds, sandhill cranes make morning and late-afternoon flights between roosting areas and feeding fields.

Breeding – Sandhill cranes begin to breed when they are 3 or 4 years old. A mating pair arrives on the breeding grounds in late spring to establish a territory.

In a spectacular mating dance, the male and female face off and jump into the air with extended wings while making noisy croaking calls. After bowing to each other, they repeat the dance.

After breeding, the mating pair builds a large, mounded nest from sticks and dead grass along the edge of a wetland. The hen lays two buff, brown-spotted eggs, which hatch in about 30 days. Both parents help tend the brood. Sandhill cranes mate for life.

Social Interaction – Sandhill cranes remain in family groups from late spring through late summer or early fall. They then gather into large migration flocks, which remain together through winter. The birds make a distinctive "kar-r-r-r-r-oo" call that can be heard up to a mile away.

Population – Sandhill cranes are separated into about a dozen different populations. Some groups are hunted and others are not, but none show signs of decline and some are increasing. The biggest threat is the loss of critical habitat along the bird's migratory routes in the central and southern United States. These birds are very long-lived and have been known to reach 19 years of age.

Hunting Strategies – Hunting for sandhill cranes is allowed in some of the Great Plains and southwestern states, usually under special permit. These birds have very keen eyesight, and pose a difficult challenge to hunters. They sometimes respond to crane decoys placed in feeding fields. Or, you can pass-shoot the birds between roosting and feeding sites. Avoid using dogs to retrieve crippled birds; the long, sharp bill can be dangerous.

Eating Quality – Young birds are considered good, but older ones are very tough and strong-tasting.

American Coot
(Fulica americana)

Common Names – Mud hen, rice hen, coot.

Description – The coot's body is dark gray to black, with a white patch on the underside of the tail. The white bill rises to form a frontal shield on the forehead. The legs and feet are yellow-green, turning red-orange in very old birds. The toes are long and thick with scalloped edges, making the birds better swimmers than the other wading birds. The sexes are identical in appearance. Juveniles are a lighter gray color, with grayish legs and a duller bill.

Size – Adults measure 13 to 16 inches long, and weigh 1 to 1¾ pounds.

Migration – The birds breed in southern and western Canada and in most of the United States, except for the southeastern states. The fall migration for northern birds begins in late August and is underway in full force by November, when the lakes begin to freeze up. Flying at night, the birds arrive on the wintering grounds in late November and December. Coots winter in much of the southern and western United States and in Mexico. Birds breeding in the southern and western states and in Mexico do not migrate.

Habitat – Coots nest on marshes, ponds and lakes fringed with emergent vegetation. They winter on the same type of habitat, but also can be found along coastal bays and inlets.

Food Habits – Coots eat a wide variety of aquatic vegetation, including duckweeds, pondweeds, milfoil, bulrushes and algae. They also eat snails and aquatic insects. Coots feed both on and below the surface, sometimes making shallow dives.

Breeding – Most birds begin breeding in their first year. The male is territorial, and aggressively patrols his breeding area to drive off intruders. After breeding, the pair builds a platformlike nest made of dead leaves and stems, anchoring it to surrounding vegetation.

The hen lays 6 to 12 tan eggs, which hatch in about 24 days. Both parents care for the young. Coots mate for life.

Social Interaction – The family group stays intact through the breeding season and into fall. Then, the group joins other families to form a large migration flock that can number as many as several hundred birds. Coots make a variety of harsh clucks, croaks, cackles and grunts.

Population – Increasing; improved water levels in the prairie pothole region are responsible for the rising numbers.

Hunting Strategies – Most coots are taken incidentally by duck hunters, but in Louisiana and other southern states, they are hunted intentionally. Coots do not respond to decoys, so the standard method involves a pair of hunters using a small boat to approach a flock in emergent vegetation – one hunter poles or rows while the other shoots at flushing birds.

Eating Quality – Fair; the dark breast meat resembles that of the stronger-tasting diving ducks.

Common Moorhen
(Gallinula chloropus)

Common Names – Florida gallinule, common gallinule, water hen.

Description – The common moorhen resembles the coot, although it is noticeably smaller and lacks the coot's distinctive, scalloped toes. In both sexes, the body is slate gray, turning brownish on the back. The sides are marked with a white stripe, and the underside of the tail is white. The bright red bill extends well up the forehead into a frontal shield, and has a yellow tip. The legs and feet are green. Juveniles are duller and more brownish than adults, and lack the colorful bill.

Size – Adults measure 12 to 14 inches long and weigh 10 to 14 ounces.

Migration – These birds breed in the eastern half of the United States, the Southwest, parts of northern Mexico, and a small portion of southeastern Canada. The fall migration begins in early October, with most birds arriving on the wintering grounds in mid- to late November. Moorhens winter in Florida, along the southern Atlantic and Gulf Coast, in much of the Southwest and in parts of northern Mexico.

Habitat – Moorhens prefer deep, freshwater marshes and ponds with some open water and dense emergent or floating vegetation, such as cattails, bulrushes and water hyacinth. They also inhabit backwater sloughs of slow-moving rivers and streams.

Food Habits – Primary foods include the leaves and stems of hydrilla and pondweed, and the seeds of smartweed, bulrushes and wild rice. The birds occasionally eat larval aquatic insects.

Breeding – Moorhens begin breeding in their first year. The birds aggressively defend their areas against rival moorhens and other birds. After breeding, the pair constructs a nest from dead vegetation among cattails or bulrushes. The hen lays 7 to 13 cinnamon-colored eggs, which hatch in about 21 days. Both parents care for the young. Moorhens often raise two broods each season.

Social Interaction – These secretive, solitary birds are seldom seen in the open, except in the fall, when they may gather in small flocks. Moorhens make a variety of squawks and croaks.

Population – Based on hunter harvest, biologists believe the moorhen population is stable.

Hunting Strategies – Most moorhens are taken incidentally by duck hunters, but some hunters jump-shoot them by push-poling small, shallow-running boats through emergent vegetation.

Eating Quality – Fair; the taste resembles that of coot.

Purple Gallinule
(Porphyrula martinica)

Common Names – Pond chicken, blue peter.

Description – The purple gallinule is slightly smaller than the common moorhen, and is much more colorful. On both sexes, the head, neck and undersides are purplish blue; the wings and back, greenish; the underside of the tail, white. The bright red bill has a yellow tip, and extends into a bluish frontal shield on the forehead. The legs and feet are yellowish. Juveniles have a brownish head, neck and undersides; an olive-colored back and wings; a dark bill; and light yellow legs and feet.

Size – Adults measure 11 to 14 inches long and weigh 8 to 12 ounces.

Migration – Purple gallinules breed in most of the southeastern states and into Mexico. Birds in the northern part of the range migrate in October, arriving in South America in December and January. Birds in Florida and along the Gulf Coast remain resident year-round.

Habitat – Purple gallinules prefer deep freshwater or brackish marshes with dense emergent and floating vegetation, such as as water hyacinth, alligatorweed, cattails and southern wild rice.

Food Habits – Common foods include sedges, wild and domestic rice, and the seeds of many types of aquatic vegetation. The birds also eat aquatic insect larvae.

Breeding – Nesting and breeding habits are nearly identical to those of the common moorhen, except that purple gallinules are less likely to have a second brood. And, unlike moorhens, purple gallinules may nest in brackish marshes.

Social Interaction – Purple gallinules are generally solitary birds, but they may gather in small flocks in fall. They make a variety of squawks.

Population – Although no population surveys have been done, biologists believe numbers are stable.

Hunting Strategies – Most purple gallinules are taken incidentally by duck or coot hunters.

Eating Quality – Fair; the meat resembles that of the coot.

Sora
(Porzana carolina)

Clapper Rail
(Rallus longirostris)

The sora is the most common North American rail. Both sexes are gray-brown, with a black face and throat, a yellow, chickenlike bill, and greenish legs and feet. Adults measure 8 to 10 inches long and weigh 2 to 4 ounces. The sora makes a distinctive, descending whinny call.

Soras breeds through much of the continental United States and southern Canada. They winter in the southern United States, Mexico and Central America.

These birds prefer shallow- to medium-depth freshwater marshes with thick stands of emergent vegetation, such as cattails and sedges. They eat duckweed, wild rice and other plant seeds, as well as insects.

The female weaves a basketlike nest from vegetation, then lays 5 to 15 eggs, which hatch in 16 to 19 days.

Most soras are taken incidentally by waterfowl hunters seeking other species. The meat is similar to that of coot.

Also known as the marsh hen, the clapper is a large, long-billed rail. Adults are 14 to 16 inches long and weigh $1/3$ to $3/4$ pound. Both sexes have a mottled grayish brown body, black-and-white barred flanks, and a white rump. The orangish bill curves slightly downward; the long legs and feet are flesh-colored. The bird's call is a harsh, "kek-kek-kek-kek."

Clappers are found primarily in coastal saltwater marshes in the Atlantic, Gulf Coast, and southern Pacific coastal states. Most do not migrate. The birds feed mainly on mollusks, crustaceans and plant seeds. The female builds a bowl-shaped nest of dead marsh grasses, then lays 9 to 12 buff-colored eggs, which hatch in 21 to 29 days.

The clapper is the most popular of the rails. The usual hunting technique involves poling boats through flooded vegetation during unusually high tides, known in the East as *marsh hen tides*. The meat is similar to that of coot.

King Rail
(Rallus elegans)

Largest of the North American rails, the king rail resembles the clapper, but has a more rusty color overall, especially in the wings and chest area. The sides are barred with black and white. Males, females and juveniles are similar in appearance. Adults measure 15 to 19 inches long and weigh 2/3 to 1 pound. The king rail's "kek-kek-kek-kek" call is identical to that of the clapper.

King rails breed mainly in the eastern United States. Most winter along the Atlantic and Gulf coast states. They prefer freshwater marshes, but in winter can also be found on saltwater marshes. King rails are especially fond of crustaceans and insects, but also eat plant seeds.

The hen builds a bowl-shaped nest from surrounding marsh grass, then lays 8 to 11 buff eggs, which hatch in 21 to 23 days.

Most king rails are taken incidentally by hunters pursuing ducks or clapper rails. The meat is similar to that of coot.

Virginia Rail
(Rallus limicola)

This small rail has rusty-colored undersides and chestnut wings. In both sexes, the cheeks are gray; the legs and bills, reddish; the rump, white. The sides are streaked with white. Adults measure about 9 inches long and weigh 2 to 4 ounces. Males are slightly larger than females. The bird makes a "ticket, ticket, ticket" call.

This rail breeds in much of the United States and southern Canada and in the northern Baja Peninsula. It winters along most coastal areas of the United States and northern Mexico. It prefers shallow, freshwater marshes with moderate stands of emergent vegetation. In winter, it is also found on brackish or saltwater marshes and estuaries. Virginia rails feed on slugs, snails and other invertebrates, as well as small fish and plant seeds.

The hen weaves a loose nest from marsh vegetation, then lays 5 to 12 pale buff-colored eggs, which hatch in about 19 days.

Most birds are taken incidentally by hunters seeking clapper rails. The meat is similar to that of coot.

Index

Cowles Creative Publishing, Inc. offers a variety of how-to books. For information write:

Cowles Creative Publishing
Subscriber Books
5900 Green Oak Drive
Minnetonka, MN 55343

Contributing Photographers

Note: T=Top, C=Center, B=Bottom, L=Left, R=Right, I=Inset

Dembinsky Photo Associates
Owosso, Michigan
©*Dominique Braud pp. 118-119*
©*Barbara Gerlach p. 45*
©*Anthony Mercieca pp. 113TL, 122TL*
©*Gary Meszaros p. 37*
©*Skip Moody p. 24I*
©*Stan Osolinski pp. 116, 121*
©*Rod Planck p. 62T*
©*Jean F. Stoick p. 74I*

Ellis Nature Photography
Portland Oregon
©*Gerry Ellis p. 57TR*

The Green Agency
Belgrade, Montana
©*Rich Kirchner pp. 9I, 44, 51, 55TR, 56, 56I, 88, 90, 90I*
©*Dale C. Spartas pp. 76T, 79, 97*

Images on the Wildside
Bozeman, Montana
©*Denver Bryan pp. 36, 42-43, 46I, 61, 78, 106-107*
©*Jim Levy pp. 102-103, 104B, 105*

Gary Kramer
Willows, California
©*Gary Kramer pp. 15I, 18-19, 47T, 50T, 53I, 58I, 81, 89, 98-99, 100, 120*

Lon E. Lauber
Wasilla, Alaska
©*Lon E. Lauber pp. 63, 77T*

Steve Maas
Minnetonka, Minnesota
©*Steve Maas pp. 92-93*

Bill Marchel
Fort Ripley, Minnesota
©*Bill Marchel pp. cover, 4-5, 6-7, 8-9, 11, 20, 21T, 27, 30, 31, 32-33, 34, 38I, 38-39, 47I, 48-49, 53B, 54T, 54I, 74-75, 82, 83, 83I, 85, 87T, 110-111*

Dr. Scott Nielsen
Superior, Wisconsin
©*Dr. Scott Nielsen pp. 12-13, 46T, 52, 55TL, 95I*

B. "Moose" Peterson
Mammoth Lakes, California
©*B. "Moose" Peterson p. 58B*

Ron Spomer
Troy, Idaho
©*Ron Spomer pp. 22, 24-25, 28-29, 87BL, 87BC, 87BR, 91, 91I, 112*

Tom Stack and Associates
Colorado Springs, Colorado
©*John Cancalosi p. 84*
©*Keith H. Murakami p. 122TR*

©*Wendy Shattil/Bob Rozinski p. 96*
©*John Shaw p. 92I*

Keith Szafranski
Livingston, Montana
©*Keith Szafranski pp. 72-73*

Bill Thomas
Missoula, Montana
©*Bill Thomas p. 77B*

U.S. Fish & Wildlife Service
Washington, D.C.
pp. 64-71

VIREO
Philadelphia, Pennsylvania
©*S. Bahrt p. 59B*
©*A. Cruickshank p. 59I*
©*Rob Curtis pp. 62I, 104I*
©*Bob de Lang p. 80*
©*S. Holt p. 95TR*
©*S. J. Lang p. 123TR*
©*A. Morris pp. 19I, 28I, 41, 123TL*
©*T. Ulrich p. 60*
©*D. & M. Zimmerman p. 57I*

Visuals Unlimited
West Swanzey, New Hampshire
©*William Grenfell p. 113TR*

The Wildlife Collection
Brooklyn Heights, New York
©*Charles Melton pp. 35, 108-109*
©*Gary Schultz p. 94T*

Lovett Williams
Suwanne, Florida
©*Lovett Williams p. 76B*

Gary Zahm
Los Banos, California
©*Gary Zahm pp. 14-15, 16-17, 40, 50I, 101, 114-115*